The Lionel FasTrack Book

Robert Schleicher

MBI

First published in 2006 by MBI, an imprint of MBI Publishing Company, Galtier Plaza, Suite 200, 380 Jackson Street, St. Paul, MN 55101-3885 USA

MBI Publishing Company titles are also available at discounts in bulk quantity for industrial or sales-promotional use. For details write to Special Sales Manager at MBI Publishing Company, Galtier Plaza, Suite 200, 380 Jackson Street, St. Paul, MN 55101-3885 USA

Library of Congress Cataloging in Publication Data
Schleicher, Robert H.
   The Lionel FasTrack book / by Robert Schleicher.
      p. cm.
   ISBN-13: 978-0-7603-2352-6
   ISBN-10: 0-7603-2352-6
      Railroads—Models—Collectors and collecting. I. Title.

TF197.S3523 2006
625.1'9—dc22

On the front cover: With FasTrack, Lionel brings the rivet-by-rivet realism of its locomotives and rolling stock right down to the rails, spike heads, ties, and ballast.

On the frontispiece: FasTrack can be arranged to create five completely separate loops so five trains run at once, each with its own transformer.

On the title page: Peter Perry's FasTrack layout fully illuminated with street and spotlights, as well as illuminated interiors in all the buildings. The locomotive headlights, the rear marker lights, and the passenger interior lighting all combine to create spectacular scenes, day or night.

On the back cover, top: FasTrack is also fully compatible with the Lionel TrainMaster Command Control system to operate five trains at once and to control switches, couplers, and operating accessories. *Bottom:* One of FasTrack's greatest virtues is ease of use. The easiest way to assemble FasTrack is on a flat tabletop. Simply push the two sections together.

About the Author
Robert Schleicher is a veteran hobby industry writer and publisher with dozens of books to his credit. His MBI titles include *101 Projects for Your Model Railroad*, *Slot Car Bible*, *How to Build and Fly Electric Model Airplanes*, and *The Big Book of Lionel*, among others.

Editor: Dennis Pernu
Designer: LeAnn Kuhlmann

Printed in China

CONTENTS

CHAPTER 1

Track Layouts for Lionel Electric Trains

The earth trembles and the air resonates with the sheer force of 6,000 horsepower moving hundreds of tons at 60 miles per hour, all guided by two relatively spindly steel rails. Lionel offers rivet-by-rivet realism of this real-life railroad action, and Lionel FasTrack carries that level of realism right down to the rails, spike heads, tie plates, ties, and ballast. Each section of FasTrack is an accurate replica of prototype track and roadbed.

Discovering FasTrack

Traditional Lionel track, with its stamped-steel ties and larger rails, has been in production for more than a century. However, any Lionel O or O-27 locomotive, freight car, or passenger car from any time in that last century will run just as well on FasTrack as on traditional Lionel track.

All of the buildings, signals, crossing gates, and streetlights are illuminated on Peter Perry's FasTrack layout.

Your local dealer can supply all the FasTrack sections and accessories you will need. You can find a listing of dealers and other information on the Lionel Web site at www.lionel.com. (The folks at Mizell Trains in Westminster, Colorado, were extremely helpful in collecting the material for this book.)

FasTrack looks just as realistic as the newest large Lionel Standard O locomotives and cars, but even tinplate Lionel trains from the 1930s, as well as the reproductions of World War II–era Lionel trains, look their best on FasTrack. An O Gauge adaptor track is available to allow you to join FasTrack to traditional Lionel O Gauge track if you want to combine both on a single layout.

Every section of FasTrack has molded-in plastic ties with realistic wood grain and simulated gray ballast designed to look exactly like loose grains of crushed rock. FasTrack sections are joined by both plastic clips and metal rail joiners for perfect alignment and reliable electrical conductivity. The FasTrack rails are shaped metal for ample current-carrying capacity and the strength to support the heaviest Lionel locomotive with ease. FasTrack also provides a quick start toward creating scenery because the built-in ballast carries the realism right to the tabletop.

Lionel enthusiasts with permanent layouts have often inserted additional wood ties and loose grains

The 72-inch FasTrack curves are large enough to provide truly realistic scenes like this one on Peter Perry's layout.

of crushed rock to make traditional stamped-steel track more realistic. But glued-down ballast and extra wood ties, changing or adding to the track was a miserable and messy operation. Now everyone has the advantage of realistic track, whether you just set up on the floor or have a permanent tabletop layout.

Because FasTrack rails, ties, and ballast are all one piece, you can change the track configuration quickly and easily to add a siding or create a double-track main line, or just create new routes. The track snaps together firmly and stays firmly connected on any reasonably flat surface.

Building Your Dream Layout

Lionel's cars, locomotives, and FasTrack are rugged enough to be used either on the floor or on a tabletop, and since FasTrack snaps together so easily and can be disassembled even easier, there's no reason why you cannot assemble a layout on the floor of a den or rec room, or even on a clean garage floor, for a few weeks of operation, perhaps at Christmas or during a long vacation weekend.

An empty 18x18-foot two-car garage floor or a similar-size basement or playroom floor is an ideal location for a large Lionel layout. There is little you can do on a permanent tabletop that you cannot do on the floor, and you can run track anywhere without worrying about whether you can reach a derailed train. If a derailment occurs, just step between the tracks (but not on the tracks), reach down, and rerail the equipment.

Certainly, placing your Lionel layout on a tabletop that is 30 to 36 inches high is the optimum location. A tabletop offers the opportunity for permanent scenery. The first question that arises, of course, is how large a tabletop? Most Lionel layouts are built on tabletops that are almost as strong as a patio deck so the operators can literally walk across the tabletop to reach derailed trains. The tabletop can be constructed from a grid of 1x4 lumber placed on edge to form 2x4-foot egg crate–style boxes with 2x4 or 2x6 legs and 1/2-inch plywood or MDF board for the tabletop. Many Lionel layout builders cover the plywood with a

sheet of 1/2-inch-thick Homasote insulating board or 1-inch-thick extruded blue or pink Styrofoam to avoid excessive noise.

One "tabletop" alternative is to build a layout on shelves that are no more than 3 feet wide (because that's about as far as you can reach). The shelves can be attached to the walls or they can be portable conference tables set up on the floor against the walls. If you have the space, you can extend one or two 6-foot-wide peninsulas from the around-the-wall portion of the layout into the room. There's an example of this type of layout on page 29 of *The Big Book of Lionel* (sold by hobby and book stores) and on page 29 of *The Lionel Train Book* (available from Lionel dealers).

A Railroad Empire in a Spare Bedroom

Many of us do not have the space for an 18x18-foot Lionel layout on either a floor or tabletop. A portable table, like a Ping-Pong table or conference table, is the solution for some model railroaders. A Ping-Pong table is just 5x9 feet, about a foot longer than a king-size bed. (In Chapter 10 you'll find plans for a range of 5x9-foot FasTrack layouts.) You can purchase Ping-Pong tables that fold onto their own platform to occupy just 2x5 feet of floor space. A table like this might be an ideal compromise if you have bedroom that is only used by guests for a few weeks out of the year.

Remember, you are not going to play Ping-Pong, so one of the 5-foot ends can go against the wall like the head of the bed. If you have a bit more room, try placing two Ping-Pong tables in a T shape for a 9x14 tabletop, or end to end for a 5x18 tabletop. I do not, however, advise placing one or two Ping-Pong tables with a 5-foot side along the wall because that would force you to reach across the 5-foot width of the tabletop to reach derailed trains.

Conference tables with folding legs are a bit more awkward to fold and store than Ping-Pong tables. Conference tables are available in a variety of sizes, however, usually in 2 1/2-foot widths and 8-, 10-, and 12-foot lengths. You can arrange a series of conference tables around the walls of a large basement room to assemble a quick and portable shelf-style layout.

Of course, you can leave your Ping-Pong or conference table(s) up more or less permanently, giving you the option of creating some permanent scenes by cutting into the table surface(s) for a river or lake.

Upgrades and Downgrades

You can create upgrades, elevated sections of track, and downgrades on a flat tabletop or even on the floor with the snap-on Lionel 12037 Graduated Trestle Set to raise the track 5 1/2-inches above the tabletop (in about 9 feet of track length) and back

Use the Graduated Trestle Set (6-12037) to build upgrades and downgrades for two-level operations with FasTrack.

down again (in another 9 feet of track length). In real railroad terms, that rise of 5 1/2 inches in 108 inches works out to a grade of 5.1 percent. You can also install the Lionel 12038 Elevated Trestle set to support the track at 5 1/2 inches above the tabletop. The Lionel trestle sets are designed to snap into the bottom of FasTrack. It is wise, however, to attach them to the tabletop with woodscrews.

It is certainly more enjoyable to have a model railroad assembled on a tabletop so you can get a trackside view of the trains from a chair rather than the floor. A tabletop layout also provides the opportunity for some permanent scenery and the wiring is easier to hide by running it beneath the tabletop.

If you have a tabletop made from 1/2-inch plywood or MDF board, you can use a saber saw to cut through the tabletop about an inch outside both edges of FasTrack. Then use blocks of 1x4s to raise the cut portions. The hollow left between the flat tabletop and elevated sections can be covered with green felt or more permanent plaster-soaked gauze like Woodland Scenics' Plaster Cloth.

Scenery for a FasTrack Layout

FasTrack features self-contained scenery, offering realism right down to the rails, tie plates, spike heads, rails, and ballast. FasTrack also gives you the option of extending the scenery out from the edges of the ballast with either portable or permanent scenery. The project layout in Chapter 5 is assembled with felt to represent the earth and flexible rocks for additional scenery. If you prefer permanent scenery, you can use plaster- impregnated gauze like that available from Woodland Scenics. Paint the dried plaster with flat latex paint and, while the paint is still wet, sprinkle on some Woodland Scenics' ground foam to simulate dirt and grass.

Plug-and-Play Electronics

Lionel's FasTrack is designed to make electrical connections as simple as possible. Lionel's three-rail system means that no special insulating gaps are required for places where trains can be reversed end-for-end, like wyes and reversing loops.

No special wiring is needed for any of the Lionel FasTrack switches. If a train enters the switch from

A FasTrack layout fully illuminated with street and spotlights, as well as illuminated interiors in all the buildings. The locomotive headlights, the rear marker lights, and the passenger interior lighting all combine to create spectacular scenes, day or night.

Bill Langsdorf elevated about half of his layout using simple 1x6 boards placed on edge. The tabletop is 3/4-inch plywood covered with a sheet of 1-inch-thick pink Styrofoam (painted green) to support the track and control the noise.

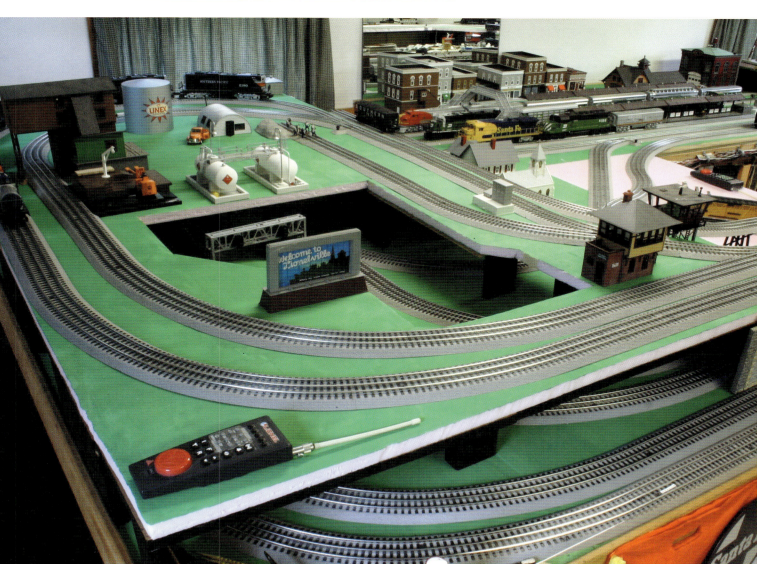

Lionel's FasTrack switches, like this 072 Remote Switch, are designed to be operated by remote control using the Remote Switch Controllers supplied with the switch.

Lionel offers several animated accessories for FasTrack, including this Track Gang (6-24105) with six moving workers and a flashing LED to simulate the welding torch.

one of the diverging routes and the switch is thrown to the other path, the Lionel FasTrack switch automatically changes direction to allow the train to travel through the switch without derailing.

Lionel FasTrack 036 switches are available with manual control, allowing you to flip a lever at each switch to change from the straight path to the curved path. All FasTrack switches are also available with electric remote control, but even the remote-control switches can be actuated manually with a lighted switch stand beside the switch.

The Lionel Switch Controllers for the remote control switches resemble the interlocking levers used on real railroads and are designed so they can be ganged together, side-by-side, like real railroad interlocking lever systems, on a control panel at the edge of your layout. Electrical wires lead from the control levers to the switches. The switch controllers are illuminated to show which direction the switch is thrown and the switch controllers can be numbered to show which switch they operate.

Operating Two or More Trains

The wiring needed to operate two or more trains using FasTrack is exactly the same as that needed with traditional Lionel track. The FasTrack sections are designed to make it far easier to connect the wires to track because each section has two or more small spades, or tabs, to accept 18-gauge quick connects. Chapter 3 contains more information on wiring a layout for operating two or more trains with conventional Lionel transformers.

FasTrack was designed to be completely compatible with Lionel's TrainMaster Command Control System, as well as with conventional Lionel transformers. The electrical spades on each track section also make it easy to attach the wires that connect the TrainMaster Command Control components to the track for operation of switches, signals, and accessories.

State-of-the-art model railroading is, in fact, best exemplified by the simplicity and realism of FasTrack combined with the electrical simplicity of multiple-train control, switch control, and accessory operation using Lionel's TrainMaster Command Control.

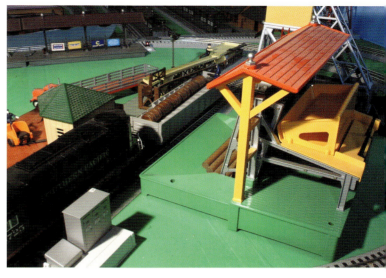

All Lionel operating accessories work perfectly with FasTrack, including the Coal Loader, Barrel Loader, Oil Drum Loader, and this AMC/ARC Log Loader (6-24115) on Bill Langsdorf's layout.

FasTrack allows you to set up a four-track mainline with 36-, 48-, 60-, and 72-inch diameter curves.

Stamped-metal Lionel accessories, either prewar originals or reproductions, operate perfectly with FasTrack. Peter Perry added a Christmas decoration to his Lionel station.

Lionel signal bridges work nicely with FasTrack, but the distance between the tracks may have to be reduced from the standard 6 inches to 4 inches by using some short filler pieces of FasTrack.

Lionel's FasTrack is designed to operate with either conventional controls or with Lionel's digital TrainMaster Command Control system.

CHAPTER 2

The Lionel FasTrack System

Lionel FasTrack combines the simplicity of three-rail with the realism of prototype railroad track, ties, and ballast. Plus, Lionel's 6-12040 O Gauge Transition Piece allows you to interface older all-steel O Gauge track with FasTrack.

The name FasTrack describes the system well enough: it is very quick to assemble and you know the joints are tight because you can hear them snap. And, those joints are nearly invisible, so you have incredibly realistic runs of apparently loose ballast for the full length of the track. The ballast, ties, tie plates, and spikes are one piece of plastic with steel rails inserted. No extra track clips and no separate track pins are needed.

The Full FasTrack Range

Lionel has produced virtually every imaginable track section for FasTrack. There are, in fact, a number of FasTrack sections that were never produced for the traditional all-metal track line in its 100 years. If you need it, the section is available; even snap-in elevated trestle sets are offered in the FasTrack line.

FasTrack must, however, fit a bit more precisely than traditional all-steel track because those FasTrack joints really need to snap to-gether tightly. The variety of short straight sections and small segment curves make it possible to obtain perfect alignment. There are some tips on getting it all right in Chapter 9.

continued on page 20

The majority of the pieces in Lionel's FasTrack series are shown here, including the 36-, 48-, 60-, 72-, and 84-inch curves; the 36-, 60-, and 72-inch switches; 45- and 90-degree crossings (center); and the variety of straight track sections.

You can use most accessories from any period in Lionel's history with FasTrack to create portable or permanent layouts.

KEY TO STRAIGHT TRACK SECTIONS ON PLANS

Symbol	Part No.	Description
BS	6-12060	Block Section (insulated 1/2-inch straight track)
BP	6-12035	Lighted Bumper
or:		
BP	6-12059	Earthen Bumper
H	6-12024	Half Straight (5-inch)
N	6-12025	4 1/2-inch Straight Track
RU	6-12054	Operating Track
S	6102047	1 3/8-inch Insulated Straight (furnished with 060 and 072 switches and as a replacement part; ballast shoulder on one side only)
SS	6-12026	1 3/4-inch Straight Track
UT	6-12020	Uncoupling Track
10	6-12014	10-inch Straight Track
45	6-12051	45-Degree Crossover
90	6-12019	90-Degree Crossover

KEY TO SWITCHES ON PLANS

Note: 060 (60-inch) and 072 (72-inch) switches are furnished with three pieces of 1 3/8-inch-long insulated straight track sections (marked S). Unless marked, all are remote control.

Symbol	Part No.	Description
36	6-12017	036 Manual Switch (Left Hand)
36	6-12018	036 Manual Switch (Right Hand)
36	6-12045	036 Remote Switch (Left Hand)
36	6-12046	036 Remote Switch (Right Hand)
60	6-12057	060 Remote Switch (Left Hand)
60	6-12058	060 Remote Switch (Right Hand)
72	6-12048	072 Remote Switch (Left Hand)
72	6-12049	072 Remote Switch (Right Hand)
Wye	6-12047	072 Wye Remote Switch

KEY TO CURVED TRACK SECTIONS ON PLANS

(Also see illustration in Chapter 9)

Symbol	Part No.	Description
C	6-12023	Half Curved Track (1/4 of 36-inch curve)
ST	6-12022	Half Curved Track; 036 22 1/2-Degree (1/2 of 36-inch curve)
T	6-12055	072 11 1/4-Degree Half Curved Track (1/2 of 72-inch curve)
36	6-12015	036 45-Degree Curved Track (36-inch curve; 8 per circle)
48	6-12043	048 30-Degree Curved Track (48-inch curve; 12 per circle)
60	6-12056	060 22 1/2-Degree Curved Track (60-inch curve; 16 per circle)
72	6-12041	072 22 1/2-Degree Curved Track (72-inch curve; 16 per circle)
84	6-12061	084 11 1/4-Degree Curved Track (84-inch curve; 32 per circle)

STRAIGHT TRACK NOT IDENTIFIED ON PLANS

Part No.	Description
6-12016	Terminal Section
6-12027	Accessory Activator Extender
6-12029	Accessory Activator Pack
6-12042	30-inch Straight Track
6-12036	Grade Crossing
6-12040	O Gauge Transition Piece
6-12054	Operating Track
6-12052	Grade Crossing with Flashers

FASTRACK ACCESSORIES

Part No.	Description
6-12039	Rerailer
6-12037	Graduated Trestle Set
6-12038	Elevated Trestle Set
6-14222	Die-Cast Metal Girder Bridge
6-24105	Operating Track Gang
6-34144	Operating Scrap Yard

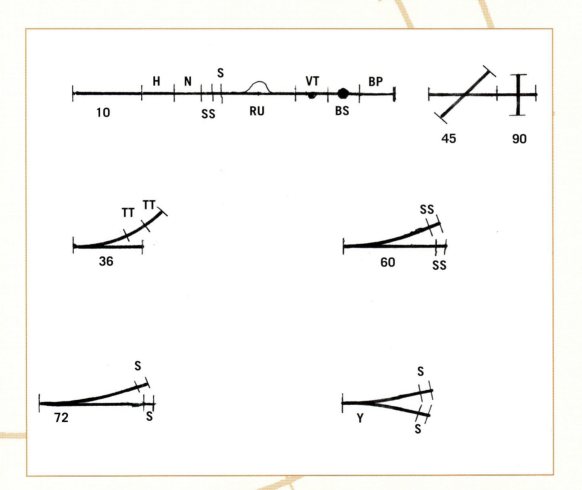

Continued from page 17
Track Plans for FasTrack

The track plans in this book use a series of common symbols and numbers to identify the specific track sections, and each plan includes a list of the total number of each track section required to recreate that plan.

The FasTrack system is designed for 6-inch spacing between tracks, as shown with this set of 72-, 60-, 48-, and 36-inch curves (left to right).

The FasTrack O Gauge Transition Piece (6-12040) can be used to join FasTrack to traditional Lionel all-steel track.

Electrical Wiring with FasTrack

Every section of Lionel FasTrack has two or more small metal tabs on the bottom of the track. You can use these to connect the wires from the transformer for either conventional "Block Control" or for TrainMaster Command Control. You can use Lionel's 6-12053 Accessory Power Wire to connect the transformer, TrainMaster, accessories, and other electronic devices to these tabs. The tabs are designed to mate with standard electronic 18-gauge snap-on quick connectors (sometimes called spade connectors because of their shape) so you can add wires by simply buying several colors of insulated 18-gauge wire, cutting it to the needed lengths, crimping the quick connectors to the wires, and snapping the quick connectors to the tabs on the underside of the track.

FasTrack Switches

The 036, 060, and 072 FasTrack switches are all available with remote control. The 036 switches are, however, also available without remote control. All of

The wired connection from the transformer on a typical FasTrack section. These 18-gauge quick connectors are attached to the power wires: one red for the center-rail power and one black for the outside-rail power return.

The FasTrack line includes track sections to operate crossing gatemen as well as graduated trestle sets or for figure-8 crossings and elevated tracks.

the switches can be operated manually by rotating the switch stand beside the track.

Remote control operation adds a bit of realism to a model railroad because you can set up one corner of the tabletop (see the layout drawings in Chapter 10) as a control tower, with all of the switch controls (and any block controls—see Chapter 3) arranged to simulate a real railroad control tower or interlocking tower. If you use TrainMaster Command Control, you can fit the 6-14182 Accessory Switch Controllers (ASC) or the 6-22980 SC-2 Switch Controller to operate the switches with a handheld TrainMaster CAB-1 Remote Control (6-12868).

A nonderailing feature is standard on all FasTrack switches. The switch is designed so that a train coming in from one of the diverging routes automatically throws the switch to the correct path. A short insulated gap is built into the inside rails of the FasTrack switches to activate this feature.

The 036 FasTrack switch is available with manual operation as shown (6-12017 left-hand or 6-12018 right-hand).

All remote control switches can also be operated manually by simply rotating the switch stand located beside the switch.

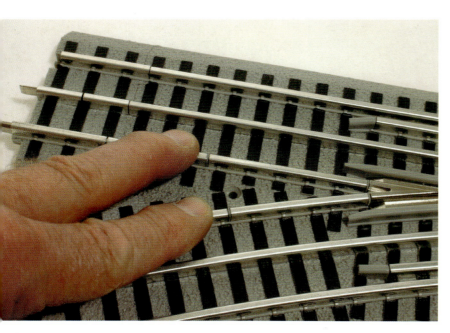

All FasTrack switches have small plastic insulating gaps on the inside diverging rails that automatically activate the nonderailing feature.

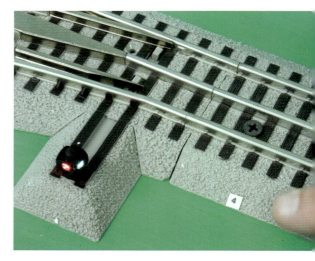

If you use the remote control lever (or if you want to operate the switches with TrainMaster Command Control), place a small number beside the switch to match the number you place inside the switch control lever's window to make it easier to identify which switch you wish to actuate.

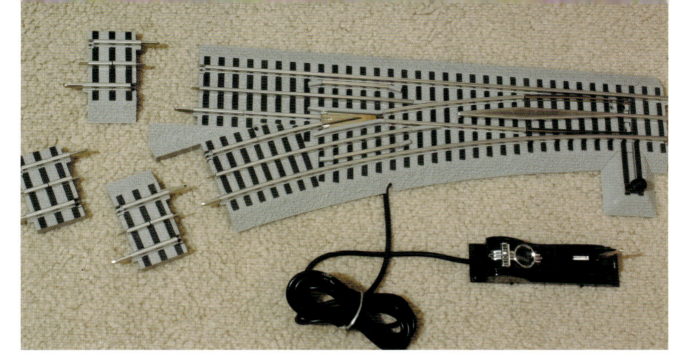

The 060 and 072 switches include three short sections of track. Any or all of the three can be used as insulated track sections (for operating two trains as described in Chapter 3) by simply unplugging the red wires beneath the track (below).

FasTrack switches include removable sections of track, making it possible to recreate plans for traditional all-steel track and providing more versatility in designing double-track main lines (like those in Chapter 7) and yards.

Relocating FasTrack Switch Stands
The switch stands that manually operate the FasTrack switches are mounted on extended platforms of simulated ballast similar to those on real railroad switches. All FasTrack switches are delivered

with these platforms on the inside or curved side of the switch because that is usually the position that provides the best clearance between adjoining tracks. In some multiple-switch layouts, however, you may want move the switch stand to the opposite side of the switch. All FasTrack switches are designed to allow this repositioning.

First, remove the two screws that retain the platform, then remove the two screws that retain the filler piece of ballast shoulder on the opposite side of the switch. Do not lose the short steel wire that lies between the ties (it's only there for appearance, however). Next, remove the platform and move it to the opposite side of the switch. Use your fingers to move the switch lever so you can see how the mechanism operates. You will note that a small pin on the switch platform engages a slot on the switch to move the switch points so the switch will change routes. That

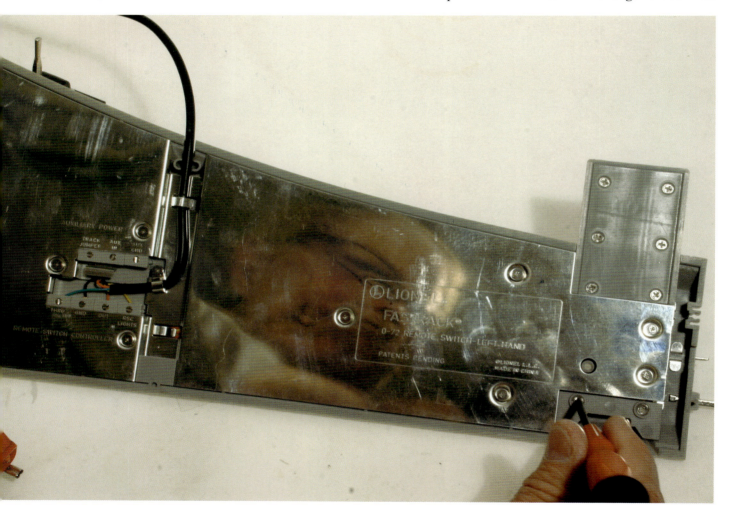

Above: To reposition the switch stand platform from the inside of the track to the outside, first remove the two screws that retain the platform.

Opposite, top: Next, remove the switch platform and lift out the short steel wire that lies between the ties. Remove the two screws that retain the filler piece of ballast shoulder on the opposite side of the switch.

Opposite, bottom: The small pin inside the switch platform engages this slot under the switch to move the switch points so the switch will change routes.

pin must engage the slot when you replace the switch platform. Line up the pin and slot as best you can, then gently wiggle the switch stand back and forth while observing to see if the switch points move as they should. Press the platform in place and double-check the manual operation of the switch. If all is well, replace the small piece of steel wire and install the two screws to hold the switch platform. Finally, install the filler piece of ballast on the opposite side of the switch with its two retaining screws.

Now line up the pin and slot, then gently wiggle the switch stand back and forth while you watch to see if the switch points actually move.

Finally, press the platform in place and double check the manual operation of the switch. Replace that small piece of steel wire and reinstall the four screws to hold the switch platform and the filler piece of ballast on the opposite side of the switch.

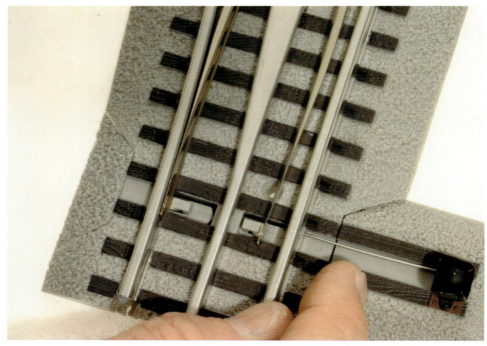

This industrial siding is from the floor-level layout in Chapter 11. The siding is long enough to have an Uncoupling Track and an Operating Track as well as storage space for three or four cars.

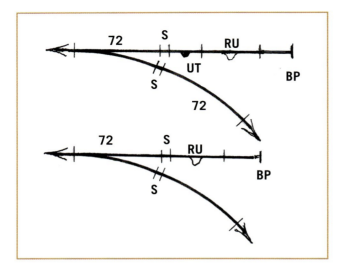

The ideal industrial siding (top) is long enough to accommodate a FasTrack Uncoupling Track (6-12020), an Operating Track (6-12054), and an end-of-track bumper (6-12035 or 6-12059). If you lack the space, the minimum siding should include (bottom) the Uncoupling Track and a bumper.

Industrial Operations with FasTrack

With FasTrack and Lionel locomotives and cars you can recreate many of the switching operations real railroads use in yards and on industrial sidings. Lionel locomotives and cars are usually fitted with automatic couplers that can be uncoupled with the remote-control electromagnet in the FasTrack 6-12020 Uncoupling Track (designated "UT" on the plans), which is the same length as a Half-Straight. Some early Lionel cars and locomotives, and some larger Lionel equipment, are fitted with automatic couplers that have small rectangular shoes that are electrically energized to activate electromagnetic coils on the couplers. These cars require a FasTrack 6-12054 Operating Track (designated "RU" on the plans—it has five rails, with an extra "operating" rail between each of the middle and outer rails) to uncouple by remote control. The 6-12054 Operating Track is the same 10-inch length as a standard straight. To uncouple the couplers automatically you need one of these two track sections at the beginning of the siding so you can uncouple the car from the locomotive. Some of the more popular Lionel automatic action cars, like

horse and milk cars, must also be used with the 6-12054 Operating Track to activate the car's action.

Finally, a dead-ended or stub-ended siding should have an end-of-track bumper so the cars are not accidentally shoved off the end of the track and derailed. Lionel makes two very realistic end-of-track bumpers (both are designated "BP" on the plans): the 6-12035 Lighted Bumper and the 6-12059 Earthen Bumper. Both are half-length straights, but the bumper itself takes up about half the length of the track section.

An ideal industrial siding would include an uncoupling track, an operating track (even if you don't yet have the operating car that would use it), and an end-of-track bumper. If you do not have that much space, then settle for the operating track, which can serve both uncoupling and operating functions, plus an end-of-track bumper.

Elevated Tracks with FasTrack

The FasTrack 6-12037 Graduated Trestle Set includes two sets of 11 simulated wood trestle bents that gradually elevate the track from the tabletop to 4 3/4 inches. Metal clips grip the edges of the ballast shoulders and snap in place. The metal clips themselves are attached to the tops of the elevated trestle

The Graduated Trestle Set (6-12037) can be used for portable layouts like those in Chapters 5 and 8, or for a permanent layout like Bill Langsdorf's in Chapter 10.

bents before the track is installed. In addition, 10-inch-long metal strips provide precise spacing for a uniform uphill grade. To assemble the Graduated Trestle Set, install the bases on each trestle, then attach the 10-inch steel spacers and the steel track clips to the top of each bent with the plastic pins. Finally, lift the track enough to slide the trestle bents beneath the track. Align the track and the Graduated Trestle bents and snap the steel clips to the edges of the track. Holes in the bases of each trestle bent allow you to attach the bent to a tabletop with 3/4-inch-long No. 4 wood screws.

If you want the track to continue around the layout at the upper level, use the 6-12038 Elevated Trestle Set that includes 10 bents, each 5 1/2 inches high. The set includes the 10-inch steel spacer bars and the steel track clips. You can also use the piers (abutments) furnished with bridges like Lionel's 6-12772 Truss Bridge with Flasher and Piers to support the elevated FasTrack as shown on the 5x9 Ping-Pong table layout in Chapter 5.

The 6-12037 Graduated Trestle Set and the 6-12038 Elevated Trestle Set are used on the 9x12 overlapping-reverse-loop layouts in Chapters 5 and 8. You can also use the Graduated Trestle set to bring the track from the tabletop to a second level, like Bill Langsdorf did on his 16x18-foot layout shown in Chapter 10.

Permanent Layouts with FasTrack

To secure the track to the table, simply insert 3/4-inch-long No. 4 sheet-metal screws into these holes and tighten them until the screw heads just touch the top of the ballast (over-tightening can distort the rails and cause derailments). The layouts in Chapter 10 have track secured to the tabletop. If you want relocate the track, simply remove the screws.

Use 3/4-inch-long No. 4 sheet-metal screws to secure the track to the tabletop, but tighten them only until the screw heads just touch the top of the ballast. Use longer screws if the tabletop is covered with 1/2-inch Homasote insulation board or 1-inch extruded Styrofoam.

CHAPTER 3

Operating Two-Trains and TrainMaster Command Control

The Lionel system is designed so you can operate as many trains as you wish, each under separate control. The easiest way to control two or more trains is to use locomotives equipped with Lionel's TrainMaster Command Control. With TrainMaster, you can operate dozens of locomotives at once, as well as switches and powered accessories, all from the handheld TrainMaster CAB-1 Remote Control.

The simplest way to operate two or three trains, however, is to assemble a layout with completely independent loops of track. If you want to run three trains at once, for example, you need three transformers. Such a layout can be a concentric set of three ovals—say, 36, 48, and 60 inches in diameter—or it can be a more complex layout, but there must be no switches to connect one loop to any other. Each train, then, has completely independent control.

Bill Langsdorf uses the Lionel TrainMaster Command Control system to operate five trains at once and to control the switches, couplers, and action accessories. Like many Lionel fans, Langsdorf likes to see a number of Lionel's action accessories grouped together in a single industrial setting.

Operating Two or More Trains with the Block System

By using conventional locomotives and power packs along with a model railroad wiring tradition called a block system, it is also possible to operate two or more trains on the same track as long as there is some place to park the train or trains that are not running. To operate two trains using the block system, add a double-ended siding (often called a passing siding) to make an oval outside a circle and you can use one end of the layout to park the train that's not running. The tracks on the siding end of the layout must be modified to electrically insulate a train-length section of track on the inner part of the oval and a second train-length siding on the outer part of the oval.

Place a piece of insulated track, either the 6-12060 Block Section ("BS" on the plans) or a piece of 6102047350 short straight from an 060 or 072

switch ("S" on the plans) on each of the diverging ends of the switches as shown in the photograph and plan. Buy two on-off switches (called SPSTs) from a hardware store. I used a heavy-duty ceramic switch intended for 115 volts outdoors because the switch itself is heavy enough to stay in place even when used for a track laid on the carpet. If you are building a permanent control panel, you can buy a panel-mount SPST switch capable of carrying at least 10 amps.

Connect the transformer to the oval end of the track (near the circled letter V), using either a 6-12016 Terminal Track or by simply plugging in spade connectors to the tabs beneath any the track sections. We will call that portion of the track "Block V."

Connect one of the on-off switches with single wire from the center rail of the inside track to the center rail of the oval on the single side of the switch near the circled letter W. This on-off switch will

Lionel's Block Section (6-12060) half-length straight offers the option of electrically insulating one or all three rails. The short straights (right) that are furnished with 060 and 072 switches also have the option of electrically isolating the center rail.

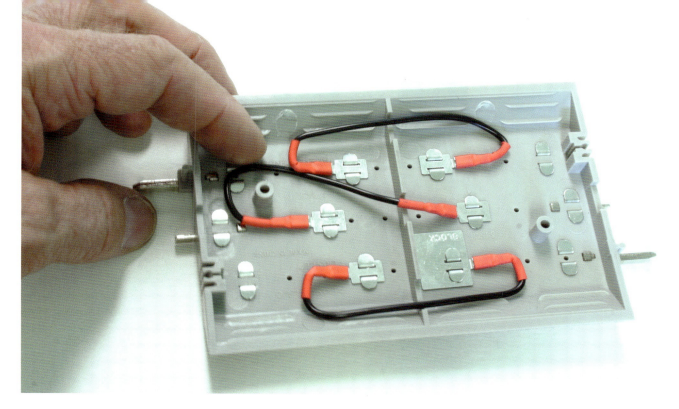

Three wires connect the rails of the Block Section. To electrically isolate any (or all) of the rails, simply unplug the red snap-on connector to the rail you wish to isolate.

A conventional Half-Straight (6-12024, at left) has no wires, but the short straights furnished with 060 and 072 switches have the option of electrically isolating the center rail by unplugging the red snap-on connectors. On the track plans in this book, solid dots indicate which of these short straights should be modified by unplugging those red snap-on connectors.

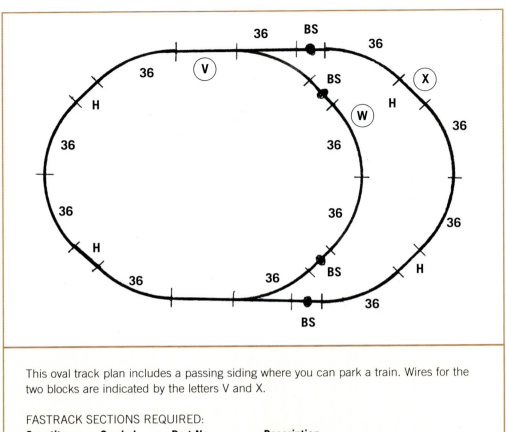

This oval track plan includes a passing siding where you can park a train. Wires for the two blocks are indicated by the letters V and X.

FASTRACK SECTIONS REQUIRED:

Quantity	Symbol	Part No.	Description
2	None	6-12014	10-inch Straight Track
4	BS	6-12060	Block Section (insulated half-straight)
4	H	6-12024	Half-Straight Track
10	36	6-12015	036 45-Degree Curved Track
1	36	6-12017	036 Manual Switch (Left Hand)
1	36	6-12018	036 Manual Switch (Right Hand)
or:			
1	36	6-12045	036 Remote Switch (Left Hand)
1	36	6-12046	036 Remote Switch (Right Hand)

SPACE REQUIRED: 4x6 feet

transfer electrical power from the main line Block V to Block W when it is turned on. When the electrical switch is turned off, no power reaches the track in the siding (Block W—the area of track between the two pieces of insulated track) and a train can be parked on that block. Connect a second on-off switch between the outer track and the main line between circled letters X and V. When that electric switch is off, a train can be parked on Block X. With both of the on-off switches set to off, neither train will run. Turn on the switch to siding Block W, and the train can be operated with the transformer. When you return that train to siding W, turn off the Block W switch. Turn on the on-off switch to siding Block X and the second train can be operated around the oval while the first train is parked in Block W.

For the simple oval with passing siding layout, only two on-off switches are needed. The wires are run from the mainline (the left half of the oval) third rail to the on-off-switch, then to the passing siding's third rail. The yellow dots (placed there only for the photograph) indicate where the Block Sections with unplugged wires are used to electrically isolate the third rails.

The transformer can be used to run just one train at a time. Turn on either of the separate black on-off switches to select which of the two trains to operate.

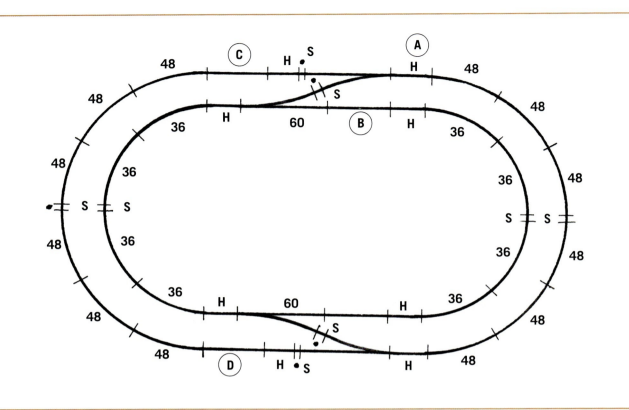

A track plan for the four-block layout. The locations of the short insulated track sections are shown by the letter S. For this layout, the suggested places to connect the wires for the four blocks are identified as A, B, C, and D. This layout utilizes 060 curves for the crossover because it's simpler to fit the short (insulated) straights and it just looks more realistic. Chapter 7 features a plan for the same layout with 036 switches.

FASTRACK SECTIONS REQUIRED:

Quantity	Symbol	Part No.	Description
4	None	6-12014	10-inch Straight Track
8	H	6-12024	Half-Straight Track
8	36	6-12015	036 45-Degree Curved Track
12	48	6-12043	048 30-Degree Curved Track
2	60	6-12057	060 Remote Switch (Left Hand)
2	60	6-12058	060 Remote Switch (Right Hand)
8	S	6102047350	1 3/8-inch Insulated Straight (furnished with 060 switches and as a replacement part; ballast shoulder on one side only)

SPACE REQUIRED: 4 1/2x7 1/2 feet

Installing a Block System on a Double-Track Main Line

You can assemble a pair of concentric ovals using 036 curves on the inner oval and 048 curves on the outer oval (or ovals with inner/outer curves of 048/060, 060/072, or 072/084 diameters). You can also connect the loops of tracks with pairs of switches to create crossovers so one train can move from the inner oval to outer oval and vice versa.

Keeping the trains apart electrically requires some special track sections to electrically isolate the layout into blocks. Each block should be a length of track long enough to hold a complete train. The length of the blocks, of course, depend on the size of the layout. For a small 36-inch oval, a block might only be three or four track sections long, just enough to hold a locomotive and two cars. On a garage-size layout, a block might be as long as 20 track sections to hold a three-unit diesel and a dozen cars or a full-length passenger train. You'll see examples of various lengths of blocks in the plans in this book.

The FasTrack 6-12060 Block Section is a 5-inch length of straight track with a built-in insulating gap in the third or center rail. Wires beneath the track are plugged into the tabs on the track to provide conventional power. To electrically insulate the section simply unplug the wires that lead to the center rail. The 060 and 072 switches include three 1 3/8-inch-long pieces of straight track ("S" on the plans) that can also be used as block sections by, again, simply

unplugging the wires leading the third rail. The short pieces have a plastic insulation piece in the center of the third rail.

Two-Train Operation with Two Transformers

This more complex two-train "block" system uses two transformers to allow you to run two trains at the same time, each on its own oval but with a pair of crossover switches (turnouts) so either train can move onto the other train's oval.

The track must be modified slightly to operate two trains at once. The first step is to install insulating track sections (with an insulating gap in the center or third rail) between each pair of switches (turnouts) at the crossovers from the inner to the outer oval to electrically isolate the inner oval (which we'll call Block B) from the outer oval at the dots marked with letter S on the plan. If you want to move the train from the inner oval (let's call it Train 2), you need to park the other train (we'll call it Train 1) on the outer oval. You then need a third electrically isolated block to park Train 1 and a fourth electrically isolated block to park Train 2. Three more insulating gaps need to be installed, as indicated by the letter S, to divide the left half of the outer oval into three blocks: the original Block C, Block D, and Block A.

This is the block wiring system used on most of the layouts in this book. The inner oval has its own on-off electrical switch (for Block B) and the outer oval is divided into three blocks—C, D, and A—each with its own on-off electrical switch. Use separate transformers to provide independent speed control for each train. Two transformers, one for the inner oval and one for the outer oval, are enough for this two-oval layout.

The wiring diagram ensures the 115-volt plugs (left) and the 18-volt wires (right) from two transformers are all wired in phase.

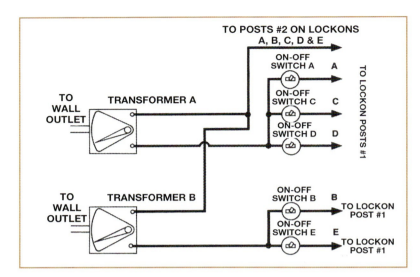

The common ground wires from both transformers are connected to the outside rail clips (post No. 2 on the old Lockons for all-steel track). The second wires from the transformers can be divided to connect any number of blocks with on-off switches (five are shown here: blocks A, B, C, D, and E). Post No. 1 on the Lockon is the metal tab beneath the FasTrack used to connect the wires with a spade connector to the center or third rail.

You can use outdoor on-off switches and wires even for a temporary layout on the floor. This simple two-oval layout is divided into four blocks with four on-off switches (only two of the on-off switches are shown here). The inner oval is Block B. The outer oval is divided into three blocks: A, C, and D. The large yellow dots indicate where the wires to the third rails are disconnected from the short straight sections to create insulated track sections.

To operate this layout, simply use one transformer to control the outer oval and a second transformer to operate the inner oval. To swap trains from the inner to the outer oval, park the first train in Block C as shown in the photos and turn off the on-off switch that directs power to Block C. The second train can then travel through the upper crossover and onto the outer oval at Block A. The second train can continue on to Block D and Block D is then turned off. Block C can then be turned on and the first train can proceed through Block B and the lower crossover to the inner oval.

If you want to use two transformers to provide independent control for two trains, the transformers must be phased so the common ground wires from both transformers are connected to the outside of each (the No. 2 posts) and the second wires from each transformer are connected to the center rail of the track. The two transformers must be wired as shown in the diagram, with the wire to Track Section A going to the center rail in Block A and the wire for Track Section B going to the center rail in Block B. The common ground wires should be joined and connected to the outer rails for *both* Block A and Block B.

Each of the two trains can circulate around its own oval under independent control with the two transformers. By parking the passenger train in Block C as shown, the freight train can be moved to the outer oval and parked in block D, on the plan. Then the passenger train can be moved to the inner oval.

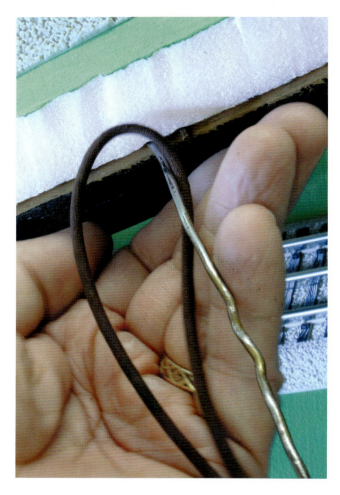

On a permanent tabletop layout, the wiring can be routed beneath the tabletop. Bill Langsdorf has 1-inch-thick pink extruded-Styrofoam on a 5/8-inch plywood tabletop. He simply punches holes through the Styrofoam with an ice pick, runs wires through holes to the edge of the table, and pulls the wires between the Styrofoam and the plywood tabletop with a hook bent in the end of a wire coat hanger.

The 115-volt wires leading to the transformers must also be phased. The wires leading to the wall plugs from each transformer must be plugged in, with the larger prong from each plug in the right-hand hole of the wall socket or extension cord. You can test the system with one of Lionel's 18-volt street lights or a simple 18-volt bulb with bare wire ends. Touch one wire from the light to Terminal A on one transformer and to Terminal A on the second transformer. If the light glows (even with transformers off), the transformers are out of phase and either wall

plug must be removed, rotated 180 degrees, and plugged back in. You can mark the plugs and sockets with a dab of paint to be sure you get them right. It's also a good idea to invest in a power strip with a surge protector to plug in all of the power packs.

The connections from the two transformers to the tabs beneath the track are made following the schematic for Transformer A and Transformer B with wires to on-off switches A through E, although for this simple two-oval example you only need Blocks A, B, C, and D (they are identified with circled letters as Blocks A, B, C, and D on the plans).

Two Trains and More with the ZW

I've shown two of Lionel's least expensive transformers controlling the double-oval trains. Lionel also offers the massive ZW and PowerHouse Power Supply Set (6-32930) that comes complete with two 180-watt power supplies and can control up to four trains. It is set so that Track 1 is controlled by the "A" handle, Track 2 by the "B" handle, Track 3 by the "C" handle, and Track 4 by the "D" handle.

The ZW transformer can also be used as a power source for Lionel's TrainMaster as shown later in this chapter. If you use TrainMaster, you can use the single hand-held CAB-1 Remote (6-12868) to control both trains.

TrainMaster Command Control

TrainMaster Command Control allows you to operate two, three, or a dozen or more trains without the electrically isolating blocks. Two trains can operate on the double oval, each under completely independent control of the other. In fact, you can run a parade of trains, each just a foot from the caboose or observation car of the next train, around any layout. All you have to watch out for is that no two trains pass through the switches (turnouts) at the same time and run into one another. That is the real thrill of TrainMaster Command Control: You are running trains, not controlling the track, which is precisely how a real railroad engineer runs his or her train. Train operation is breathtakingly realistic with the TrainMaster system.

The CAB-1 Remote for the TrainMaster system is a wireless remote, just a bit larger than a typical television

The TrainMaster CAB-1 Remote Control (6-12868) is used to operate Lionel trains; speed is controlled by the red knob, while direction, sound, and other functions are controlled by the buttons. CAB-1 can also be used to control switches. Bill Langsdorf identifies his switches with numbers.

remote control. Since there are no wires, you can walk along beside your train or sit back in an easy chair and run the layout from the "tower." The CAB-1 Remote has a knob to control speed, a "panic button" (labeled "Halt") to stop the trains, a reverse switch, a series of buttons to activate RailSounds and other accessories, and a set of numbered buttons so you can dial up the number of each locomotive you want to control.

If you want to run two diesels back-to-back in what the real railroads call "multiple-unit lash-ups" (MUs, for short), you can program each locomotive to perform exactly like its mate. The two can then be coupled together and the TrainMaster system will keep them operating at identical speeds relative to one another so when one speeds up, the other matches it precisely. You can also program the locomotives for longer duration of acceleration or braking to simulate heavier loads.

Locomotives and cars equipped with Lionel's ElectroCouplers can be uncoupled anywhere on the track at the push of a button on the CAB-1 Remote. For conventional Lionel operating couplers, the hand-held CAB-1 Remote can be used to actuate the FasTrack 6-12020 Uncoupling Track or 6-12054 Operating Track to uncouple cars or locomotives on these track sections (or to activate automatic cars that dump or have other animation).

If you have Lionel's RailSounds, the CAB-1 Remote also gives you full control of steam locomotives whistles, bells, and exhaust sounds, and diesel locomotive horns, bells, and engine growls. Many conventional Lionel locomotives also have RailSounds and those can, of course, be actuated through conventional Lionel transformers (or you can use the TrainMaster for conventional locomotives equipped with RailSounds, if you wish). Additional buttons control sound effects like clanging couplers and lowing cattle, as well as track switches, lights, action cars (including uncoupling and unloading), and accessories like log loaders and magnetic cranes. Your entire Lionel world is under your fingertips with your CAB-1 Remote.

How TrainMaster Works

There are five basic components for the Lionel TrainMaster Command Control System:

1. A locomotive equipped with a built-in TrainMaster Command Control Receiver;
2. A power supply with at least 18 volts (a large Lionel transformer or a Lionel 180-Watt PowerHouse Power Supply [6-22983]);
3. A TrainMaster Command PowerMaster 135 (6-12867), a TMCC Track Power Controller 300 (6-14189), or a TMCC Track Power Controller 400 (6-14179);
4. A Command Base (6-12911); and
5. The CAB-1 Remote Controller (6-12868).

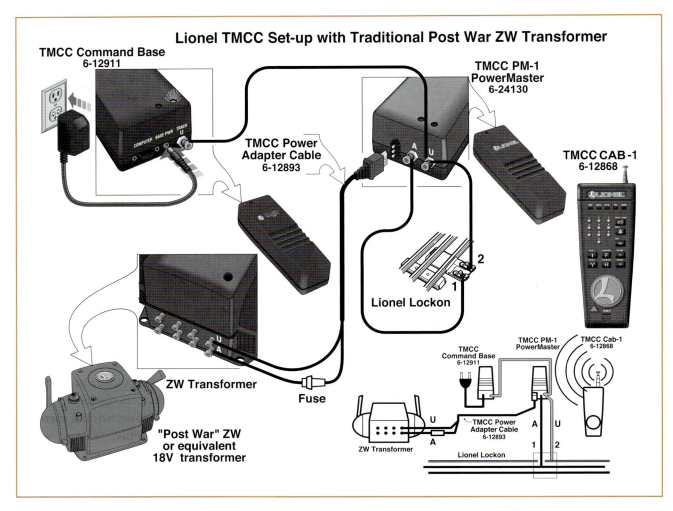

Lionel TMCC Set-up with Traditional Post War ZW Transformer

TMCC Command Base
6-12911

TMCC PM-1 PowerMaster
6-24130

TMCC Power Adapter Cable
6-12893

TMCC CAB-1
6-12868

Lionel Lockon

ZW Transformer

Fuse

"Post War" ZW or equivalent 18V transformer

TMCC Command Base 6-12911

TMCC PM-1 PowerMaster

TMCC Cab-1 6-12868

TMCC Power Adapter Cable 6-12893

ZW Transformer

Lionel Lockon

TrainMaster Command Control Wiring with Traditional Postwar ZW Transformer. *Courtesy Lionel LLC*

Lionel's TrainMaster Command Control supplies a steady 18 volts to the rails; the speed control is inside the locomotive, activated by signals from the CAB-1 Remote. The system uses radio control transmitted from the CAB-1 Remote to tell the receiver inside each TrainMaster-equipped locomotive to speed up, slow down, or reverse, and each of those functions is adjustable. An antenna inside each locomotive (or, in some cases, handrails serve as antennae) and the outside rails relay the signals to the receiver inside the locomotive.

The wiring diagrams show how to connect a conventional Lionel transformer like the postwar ZW or the new TrainMaster PowerHouse Power Supply to the track. These systems allow you to run either TrainMaster-equipped locomotives or any conventional Lionel locomotive from the past 100 years (the really low-priced locomotives were DC and must be converted to AC by your Lionel Service Station). Virtually every other locomotive Lionel ever made (and most other brands of locomotives intended for three-rail Lionel track) will run with the TrainMaster system.

If you use the ZW exclusively to provide power for the TrainMaster Command Control system (TMCC), turn off the ZW when you are through running trains. When you start up the system for the next operating session, give the Command Base and any other transformers a minute to come online before turning on the ZW.

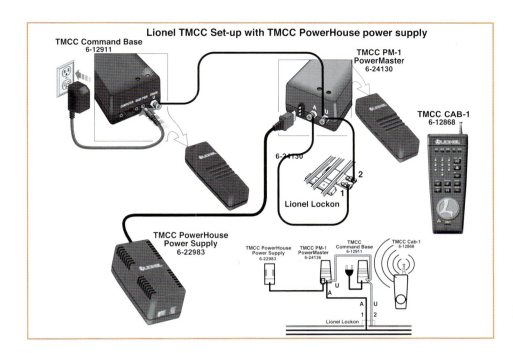

Lionel TMCC Set-up with TMCC PowerHouse power supply

TMCC Command Base
6-12911

TMCC PM-1
PowerMaster
6-24130

6-24130

TMCC CAB-1
6-12868

Lionel Lockon

TMCC PowerHouse
Power Supply
6-22983

TMCC PowerHouse
Power Supply
6-22983

TMCC PM-1
PowerMaster
6-24136

TMCC
Command Base
6-12911

TMCC Cab-1
6-12868

Lionel Lockon

TrainMaster Command
Control Setup with TMCC
PowerHouse Power Supply.
Courtesy Lionel LLC

Below: TrainMaster
Command Control Setup
for Use with TrainMaster-
Equipped Locomotives
Only. *Courtesy Lionel LLC*

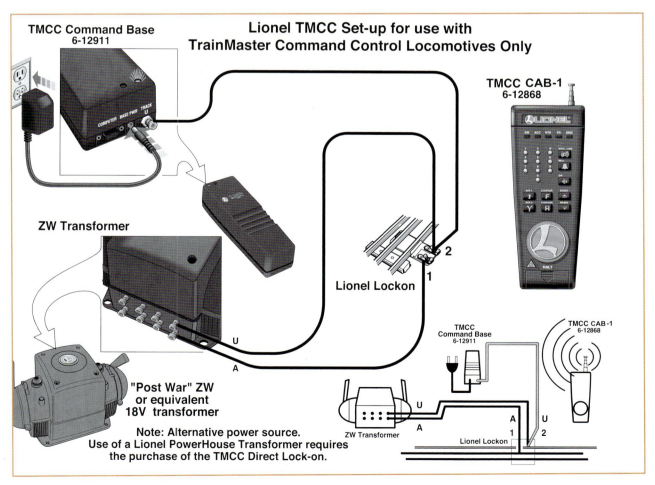

**Lionel TMCC Set-up for use with
TrainMaster Command Control Locomotives Only**

TMCC Command Base
6-12911

TMCC CAB-1
6-12868

ZW Transformer

Lionel Lockon

"Post War" ZW
or equivalent
18V transformer

Note: Alternative power source.
Use of a Lionel PowerHouse Transformer requires
the purchase of the TMCC Direct Lock-on.

TMCC
Command Base
6-12911

TMCC CAB-1
6-12868

ZW Transformer

Lionel Lockon

If you have only TrainMaster equipped locomotives, you can skip the PowerMaster and use the wiring diagram shown here with a powerful 18-volt transformer like Lionel's massive postwar ZW.

If you use Lionel's PowerHouse Power Supply in place of the ZW transformer, you will also need to use Lionel's special 6-34120 TMCC Direct Lockon that uses a small equipment shed to house the necessary circuit breaker and electronics. Connect wires from the tabs of the Lockon to the tabs for the rails beneath the track. Most of us, however, will want to operate at least one conventional Lionel locomotive, so simply plugging the spade connections directly to the tabs beneath rails is fine. Conversely, any Lionel locomotives equipped with TrainMaster can also be operated with conventional Lionel controls.

The TrainMaster system needs at least an 80-watt transformer. If you are operating some of the larger locomotives or running two or more locomotives, you may need even more power than the 135 watts delivered by the Lionel 6-12866 PowerHouse Power Supply. Lionel also offers a larger 180-watt 6-22983 PowerHouse Power Supply, of which you may need two or more. Neither the 135-watt or the 180-watt PowerMaster transformers have the special circuit breakers needed so you must be sure to use the 6-24130 135/180-watt Switchable Power Master, the 6-14189 Track Power Controller 300 (for two 135-watt or one 180-watt PowerHouse Power Supplies), or the 6-14179 Track Power Controller 400 (for two 180-watt PowerHouse Power Supplies) to allow operation of both conventional and TrainMaster

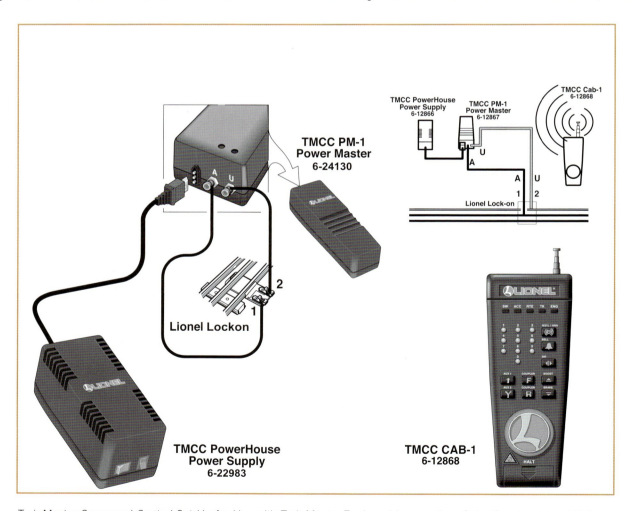

TrainMaster Command Control Set-Up for Use with TrainMaster-Equipped Locomotives Only. *Courtesy Lionel LLC*

This is a TMCC Direct Lockon (6-34120). Bill Langsdorf uses small numbers to identify which part of his layout is connected to which Direct Lockon.

The Lionel ZW and PowerHouse Power Supply Set (6-32390) can be used to run two conventional trains. Bill Langsdorf uses his to provide power for the accessories on his large layout shown in Chapter 10.

The control center on Bill Langsdorf's large TMCC-equipped Lionel layout includes one Track Power Controller (TPC) 400 (6-14179), one Track Power Controller (TPC) 300 (6-14189, the XTPC3000 from IC Controls), one TMCC Command Base (6-12911), and five TrainMaster Command PowerMasters (6-24130).

locomotives (or use the 6-34120 Direct Lockon if you are running *only* TrainMaster-equipped locomotives). Lionel recommends connecting additional feeder wires beneath the track to the center and outside rails, with or without blocks, every 6 feet of track.

If your model railroad is larger than about 5x9 feet, you should divide it into blocks as described earlier for conventional two-train operation. You don't need all the on-off switches with TrainMaster; just unplug the center rail wires from the short straight track sections (S on the plans) to provide the insulating gaps in the third rail, and plug in power wires to the third rail tabs beneath the track to connect to the TrainMaster system as shown in

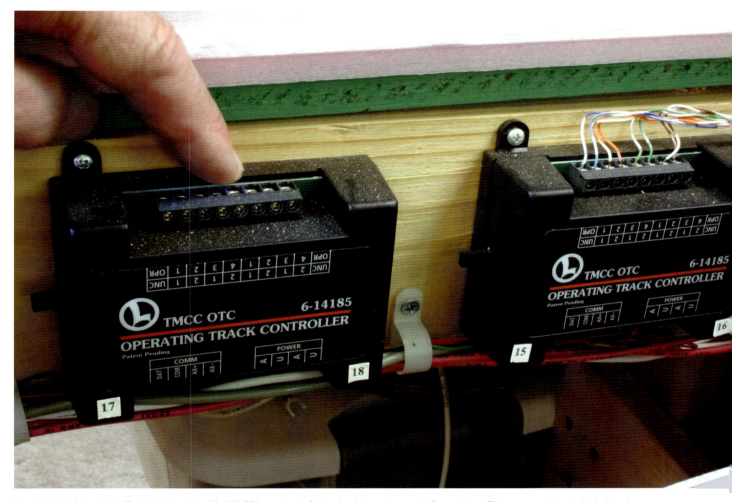

The TMCC Operating Track Controller (6-14185) on the left is wired into Langsdorf's system. The one on the right is in place, ready for wire connections on the layout.

the diagrams. The blocks provide better electrical current flow and make it easier to isolate any short circuits that might occur from a derailed set of wheels. You will need a 6-12867 Power Master, a 6-24130 Track Power Controller 300, or a 6-14179 Track Power Controller 400 for each block.

It's wise to protect each portion of a large layout with the TMCC Direct Lockon (6-34120). If you are operating TrainMaster on a large layout, you may want use several TMCC Direct Lockons. Bill Langsdorf uses five on his 16x18-foot layout (see Chapter 10), one for each track, for full over-current protection with an automatic reset.

Langsdorf also uses singular 18-gauge color-coded wire for all track connections: red for hot power, black for ground power, white for signal returns, and green for accessories. The track wires are connected to a TMCC 6-34120 Direct Lockon for each of the five loops of track. The wires lead from the track to terminal strips, then to the various power supplies. Langsdorf uses 22-gauge white-jacketed four-wire (red, green, black, and yellow) to wire accessories. These wires are also connected from the accessories to a terminal strip, which is connected to a power supply. He gangs the wires into neat cables contained in 1/2-, 1-, and 2-inch plumbing pipe holders. He uses electrical wire markers for each individual wire for proper identification as well as to identify individual switch, individual engine, and individual accessory numbers. The numbers are necessary because they are the numbers you must keypunch when using a CAB-1 Remote to control the layout.

(On the same note, if you are assembling a large Lionel layout, it is wise to organize the TMCC components into specific areas with labeled and color-coded wiring, using plastic pipe holders to organize and collect the wires.)

Lionel also offers an intriguing 6-14181 TMCC Action Recorder Controller that allows you to program up to eight actions automatically. You can, as a simple example, have a train stop at a log loader, dump its load of logs, and proceed around the track to the back side of the log loader to be reloaded with logs, with just the touch of a single button.

If two or more friends want to operate trains at the same time, you can use additional CAB-1 Remotes for each of their trains. You may also need to purchase additional power controllers and, perhaps, more transformers to provide the power to run three or more trains at once.

TrainMaster to Control the Entire Layout

Lionel offers a variety of electronic components for the TrainMaster system so the CAB-1 Remote can be used to activate different sounds or puffs of simulated steam or smoke, to turn lights on or off, and, with trackside control receivers called Controllers, to actuate switches, turn blocks on or off, uncouple cars, activate

This is the track power area on Bill Langsdorf's layout. It contains three 180-Watt PowerHouses (6-22983) and five 135-Watt PowerHouses (6-12866). The 180-Watt PowerHouses are used on the TPC3000s: one on Track 1 and two on Track 2. The 135-Watt PowerHouses are used for Tracks 3, 4, and 5. The last two 135-Watt PowerHouses are for future expansion.

action cars, activate action accessories, even increase or decrease the brightness of lights—all with the push of a button.

If your layout is controlled by the TrainMaster system, you can control the blocks from the buttons on the CAB-1 by wiring the blocks through the Block Power Controller (6-14184). Using the Accessory Motor Controller (6-14183), the CAB-1 can also be used to control accessories with speed changes. If you want to set a speed on an accessory, use the Accessory Voltage Controller (6-14186). To actuate the Remote Control Uncoupling Track to dump loads, activate other operating cars, and operate automatic uncouplers, use the Operating Track Controller (6-14185).

Due to the system's internal complexity, Lionel does not offer conversion kits for locomotives that are not factory-equipped with TMCC.

Tips for TrainMaster Command Control

On metal bridges, an earth ground wire may be necessary to prevent false TMCC signals or the loss of a TMCC signal while the train is running through a bridge, or if another train is running beneath the bridge. When there is a loss of signal, the TMCC engines' lights begin to flicker. The earth ground on bridges prevents this.

When TrainMaster Command Control locomotives are in a block that is in an electrically isolated or a stop section, the programming can be lost if the

To prevent loss of signal with TMCC you may need to install an extra earth-ground wired to the frame of the bridge like this Hell Gate Bridge on Bill Langsdorf's layout.

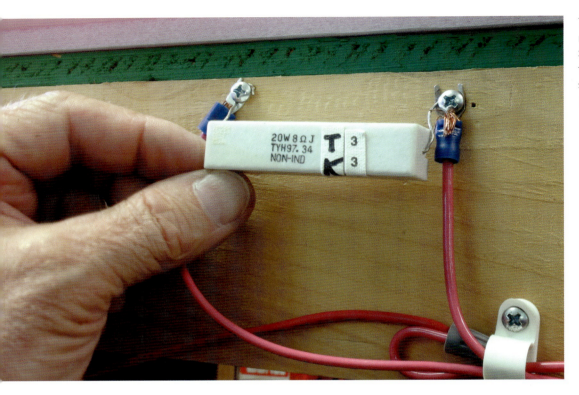

This is a 20-watt 8-ohm resistor (available at Radio Shack) that can be used to allow TMCC engines to stop without losing their program settings.

power is shut off completely to that portion of the track. If a 20-watt, 8-ohm resistor (available at Radio Shack) is installed in the wire leading to track, the resistor will allow the locomotives to stop completely but still have enough power to retain their program-ming. The resistor allows 7 volts to stay on the track for the Command Control functions to operate. When full power is restored to the track, the Command Control locomotive will resume the same operating speed that was programmed before it stopped.

Automatic Uncoupling and Accessory Operation

Lionel uses two different styles of couplers. The most common design has a small metal disc suspended beneath the coupler. To uncouple the coupler, the car is parked over a section of track with an electromagnet. When the magnet is energized, it attracts the steel disc, pulling it downward, opening the coupler knuckle, and uncoupling the car. Many of the action cars, like the mail car, log-dump car, and coal-dump car, have similar steel discs that allow them to be operated by the electromagnet. The Lionel half-straight 6-12020 Uncoupling Track operates the couplers and action cars. Some of the older Lionel cars and locomotives are fitted with couplers that have their own built-in electro-magnets. These couplers are actuated electrically through small rectangular shoes on the bottoms of

Bill Langsdorf installed a Radio Shack TP-900 Universal Antenna in place of the standard aerial on his TrainMaster Cab 1 remote.

On a layout as large and complex as Bill Langsdorf's, the electrical components and wiring must be organized. His control board includes TMCC SC-1 (6-12914) and SC-2 (6-22980) Switch Controllers, along with double-pole-double-throw (DPDT) 12-volt block relays used in place of on-off switches to control power to the blocks. There are also Action Recorders Controllers (6-14181), Accessory Motor (ASC300), and Operating Track Controllers (6-14185).

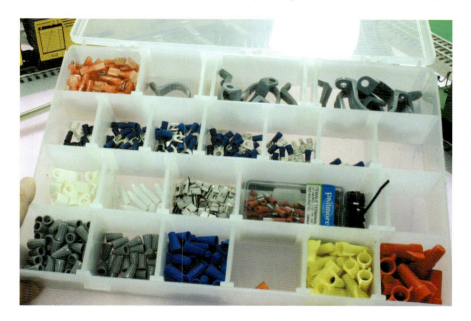

Bill Langsdorf keeps a divided plastic tray with crimp-on spades for 18- and 14-gauge wire (to plug wire into the metal tabs beneath each FasTrack section), connectors for joining wires, cable ties, and pipe holders.

the trucks that receive a signal from a fourth and fifth rail. The Lionel 6-12054 Operating Track is fitted with these fourth and fifth rails to actuate the couplers. Also, some of the action cars, like the Operating Milk Car, are actuated by a similar type of shoe and require the 6-12054 Operating Track. The 6-12054 Operating Track also has its own electromagnet (like the 6-12020 Uncoupling Track) so it can be used to operate cars with steel discs for uncoupling or action operation as well.

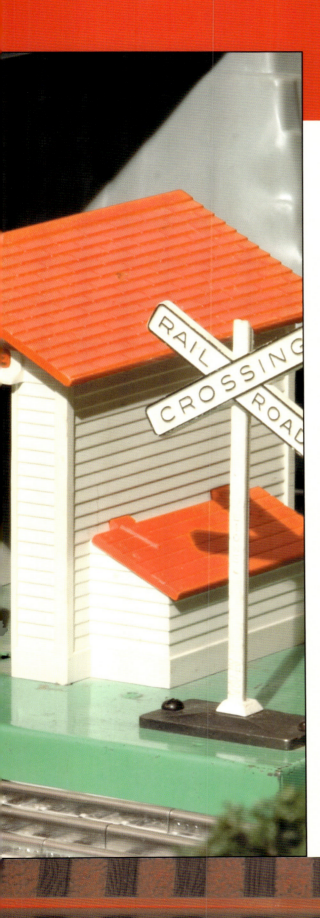

CHAPTER 4

Track and Accessories

The FasTrack system is designed to be easy to use but complete enough so you can create the most complex layouts in the history of Lionel trains. Any O or O-27 locomotive, freight car, or passenger car will operate perfectly on FasTrack, usually even smoother than on traditional all-steel track. The same wiring techniques are used with FasTrack as with traditional Lionel products. In this chapter, I'll describe some wiring tips for switches and accessories. I suggest you review the wiring tips and techniques in *The Big Book of Lionel Trains* or *The Lionel Train Book* for more information on operating Lionel layouts. There is also information in Chapter 3 on wiring a Lionel layout to operate two trains or more with either conventional block control or with TrainMaster Command Control.

FasTrack is designed to allow the use of most of the newest and oldest Lionel accessories, including a classic Automatic Gateman.

Assembling FasTrack

It is easiest to assemble FasTrack on a flat tabletop or floor where you can slide the sections together. The steel pins provide alignment and small plastic tabs beneath the track provide the grip to hold the track sections together. Grip the ballast shoulders and push the two sections together until you hear the click that indicates the locking tabs are seated in their sockets. You can also see that track is assembled perfectly because there should be no visible gap between the sections. Stand 10 feet away and you should not even be able tell where the joints are located. The ballast edges are rough, of course, so you may want to wear some cotton gardening gloves if you are assembling a large layout.

FasTrack Maintenance

You can use the same cleaning fluid and eraser to clean FasTrack that you would to clean the traditional all-steel track. Lionel's Lubrication/Maintenance Set (6-62927) includes both cleaner and eraser. First, wipe the track clean, then apply some of the cleaning fluid to a clean rag and wipe the surfaces of the rails. If there are stubborn deposits, polish those areas with the track-cleaning eraser. Never scrape the surface of the track with a knife because you can leave scratches that will attract more dirt and oxide. And never, ever use steel wool to clean anything on a model railroad. The small fibers will be attracted by motor magnets, and if they work their way into the motor, they can create a short circuit that can burn out the motor.

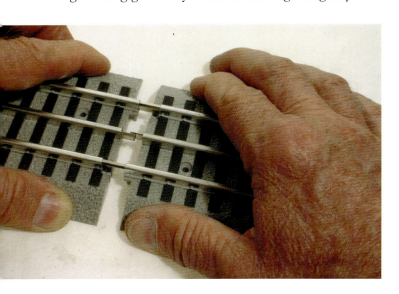

Above: The easiest way to assemble FasTrack is on a flat tabletop. Simply push the two sections together.

Above, right: Vertical pencil lead–size plastic pins and matching C-shaped notches provide the "snap" that holds the FasTrack sections together. The metal pins provide alignment and carry the electrical current.

Right: If you are assembling dozens of pieces of FasTrack, wear cotton gardening gloves so you can push the track sections firmly together without wearing out your fingertips.

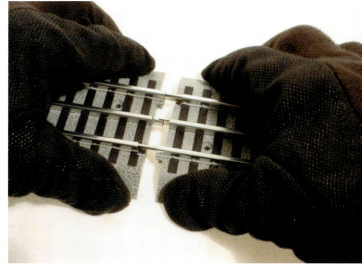

Usually, the track can be wiped clean with a lint-free rag. If the dirt is stubborn, dampen the rag with the track-cleaning fluid from the Lubrication/Maintenance Set (6-62927). Always work in a well-ventilated area when using the fluid.

If the track will not wipe clean, you can scrub it with the track-cleaning eraser from the Lionel Lubrication/ Maintenance Set.

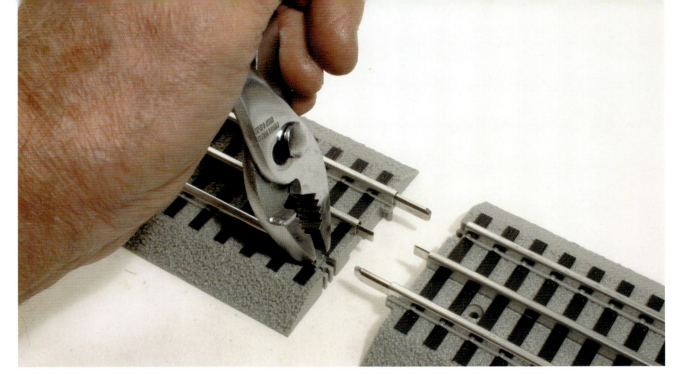

If the track joints are worn loose from hundreds of assembly/disassembly cycles, you can tighten them by squeezing the sides of the rail with pliers. Do not try to squeeze the rails without the track pins inside or you may crush the steel and permanently damage the rails.

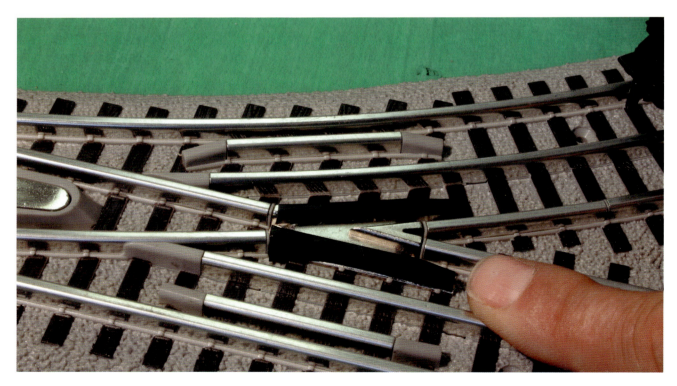

The first production series of 036 manual switches were fitted with metal frogs that can cause locomotives to stall. Newer ones have plastic frogs like the remote control switches. You can correct the problem by simply covering the frog area with black electrical tape as on this switch on Bill Langsdorf's layout.

Lionel remote switch controllers are designed to recreate the look and feel of the switch levers in a real railroad's interlocking tower.

If you have not operated for several months, gently rub over the tops of all the rails with the track-cleaning eraser to scrub away any oxides and residue for perfect electric contact, then wipe the rails with a clean cloth. You can, of course, also use the fluid and eraser to clean locomotive wheels and the third-rail electrical pickup rollers.

FasTrack is rugged but you can damage the track if you step on it or if you try to pick up a half-dozen pieces that are still snapped together. Usually the damage is limited to the steel rails being forced apart by the steel track pins. If the track pins do not fit tightly inside the hollow steel rails, trains can derail and electrical current flow can be erratic or not flow at all. You can tighten the rails around the track pins with common pliers. Just squeeze the base of the rail firmly so it closes tightly around the track pins. Do not try to squeeze the rails without the track pins inside or you may crush the steel and permanently damage the rails.

Wiring FasTrack Switches

Lionel remote switch controllers are designed to recreate the look and feel of the switch levers in a real railroad's interlocking tower. Just flick the lever and the track switch changes from the straight to the curved route or back again. The control boxes snap together side by side and are illuminated red for the siding and green for the straight to match the position of the rotating switch stand beside the track. The round windows display an illuminated disc of replaceable numbers so you can identify the switch. Some modelers use small sticky labels to apply the matching number to the ballast shoulder beside the switch and make it easier to be sure the switch lever is throwing the switch they want thrown.

If you need to extend the wires' length, you can remove the four wires, splice in the necessary length of wire, and reconnect the now longer wires. However, there is a better way. Purchase a 12-position terminal strip like the Radio Shack No. 274-677. Mount the terminal strips to the edge or top of the table near the transformer and switch controllers. Run the extra extension lengths of wires from the switches to the terminals on one side of the terminal strip. Connect the Lionel FasTrack Switch Controller wires to the terminals on the opposite side of the terminal strip, which is used as the splice point to extend the wires, and the terminal strip will help to keep the wiring more organized. As mentioned in Chapter 3, Bill Langsdorf uses 22-gauge white-jacketed four-wire

(red, green, black, and yellow) cable for the extended wire runs. The colored wires are then connected to the posts on one side of the terminal strip, and the original switch control wires are connected to the matching posts on the opposite side of the terminal strip.

The remote-control switches can pick up their power from the rails. Or you can supply a separate power source from the fixed-voltage outlets on the transformer or, better yet, from a separate transformer. On the bottom of every switch there are three screw terminals marked "Auxiliary Power." Loosen the two right screws and remove the metal jumper tab. Insert the wires from the separate power supply in the terminals marked "Aux. Ground" and "Aux. In" and tighten the screws.

Installing Lionel Action Accessories

All Lionel action and operating accessories, including coal conveyors, log loaders, and magnetic cranes, can be used with FasTrack. Some of these accessories

Use a small Phillips-head screwdriver to loosen the terminal screws to remove the switch-control wires from the bottom of the remote control switches.

Extend the length of wire from switches to operating levers by installing the extra lengths of 22-gauge wires to the bottom of the switches, then splicing the wires to the original levers' wires.

Some operating accessories will function correctly when placed at the edge of the FasTrack ballast shoulders, as on Bill Langsdorf's layout.

must be located at the edge of the ties, closer than the ballast shoulders on FasTrack will permit. The FasTrack 6-12054 Operating Track (the one with five rails) has a removable ballast shoulder for this purpose, but not all accessories require this special track section. If you need to move the action accessory closer to the track, use a hacksaw to simply saw off the ballast shoulder from a piece of 10-inch straight track.

Train-Actuated Signals and Crossing Gates

Lionel has offered dozens of two-bulb searchlight signals and drop-arm semaphore signals over the years, and all Lionel signals and crossing gates can be used with FasTrack.

One of the many advantages of the three-rail track system is that you can use one of the rails as a trigger to control signals, warning devices like the Automatic Gateman, and Crossing Gates. With the 6-12029 Accessory Activator FasTrack section, there is no need for special contacts or switches; just replace two standard straight sections with a pair of Accessory Activator track sections.

Lionel offers the 6-12029 Accessory Activator FasTrack in a package with a full-length insulated track and two half-length insulated straights. The total length of the insulated portion of the track is about 15 inches. If you need a longer length for really large locomotives, additional 10-inch insulated track

Above: Most operating accessories will operate beside any FasTrack section, including this 97 Electric Coaling Station (6-32921) and the Rotary Aircraft Beacon (6-14097) in the background.

Above, right: Most vintages of Lionel accessories can be used with FasTrack, including items like this circa-1940 No. 165 Magnetic Crane on Peter Perry's layout.

Right: The Illuminated Fueling Station (6-12877) and an Illuminated Station Platform (6-12748) do not need to be any closer to the track than the edge of the standard FasTrack ballast shoulder.

Some operating accessories need to rest against the ends of the ties. Use an Operating Track (6-12054) section and remove the ballast edge, or use a hacksaw to trim the ballast edge from a standard straight.

An Operating Icing Station (6-12847) rests against a FasTrack standard straight with ballast edge removed.

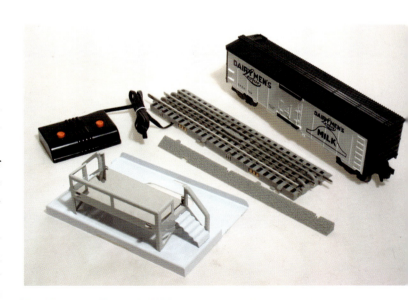

The Operating Track (6-12054) section has fourth and fifth rails for operation of some types of Lionel couplers and operating cars like this Operating Milk Car. The Operating Track section has a removable ballast shoulder to allow accessories like the platform for the Operating Milk Car to rest against the edges of the ties.

sections are available as number 6-12027 Accessory Activator Extenders. The Accessory Activator is merely a single piece of track with metal strips that connect to the outside rails removed. The outside rail can now serve as a contactor to activate any warning accessory. Remember that the insulated rails of all the track sections in the Accessory Activator pack and any additional Accessory Activator Extender tracks must be on the same side of the track to leave the rail on the opposite side open to provide power for the locomotives.

The passing of the locomotive closes the circuit between the power from the third rail and the power from the electrically isolated rail. Because both outside rails provide the same electrical power, one of those rails is free to be used as an Accessory Activator track section without affecting the flow of electricity to the locomotive in any significant manner.

Install the Accessory Activator by simply replacing pieces of track. For some devices, like the Automatic Gateman, two track power wires are needed; plug these into the tabs on the unmodified rails on the bottom of track section on either side of the single insulated rail. The Accessory Activator Track leaves no electrical connection to the insulated portion of the track section. The passing locomotive provides a connection between the insulated rail and the first electrical connection to turn on the device and a second contact between the second electrical connection and the insulated rail to turn off the device. There are no moving parts with this system. All you need are clean rails, which you want in any case.

Although you can pick up power from the track, each Lionel signal or crossing-warning device should be supplied with its own power. It's best to have a separate power pack so the accessory does not affect the operation of the trains (and vice versa). The accessories usually have three wires: a ground, a wire to provide power, and a third wire to actuate the solenoid, coil, motor, or electronic chip that operates the device.

If you run trains in both directions, you may want to install Accessory Activators a foot or so on both the right and left of the signal or crossing warning device so that it is properly actuated by trains traveling in either direction.

Control by Infrared Light

Lionel offers a third option to control signals and warning devices. The 153IR Controller (6-14111) looks like a trackside maintenance shed, but it houses an infrared detector that can be adjusted for time delay from 0 to 20 seconds. There is no need to attach anything to the track or to use special track sections. Just position the 153IR Controller near the edge of the ballast shoulder and run the wires to the signal or crossing gate and to the power supply.

The 153IR is the simplest method of providing control for signals, but on a layout with dozens of signals to be controlled, you may want to alternate between installations of the 153IR Controller and the Accessory Activator insulated track sections, especially if you want the signal or crossing warning device to be actuated by trains traveling in either direction.

The all-metal Double Automatic Crossing Gates on Peter Perry's FasTrack layout are from the 1937 Lionel line.

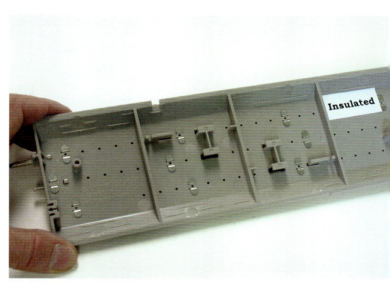

The half-straights in the Accessory Activator Pack (6-12029) have this molded-in piece of plastic to provide an insulated gap in one outside rail.

Because the Accessory Activator track has an insulated outside rail, there are no metal connectors from the one outside rail to the opposite outside rail.

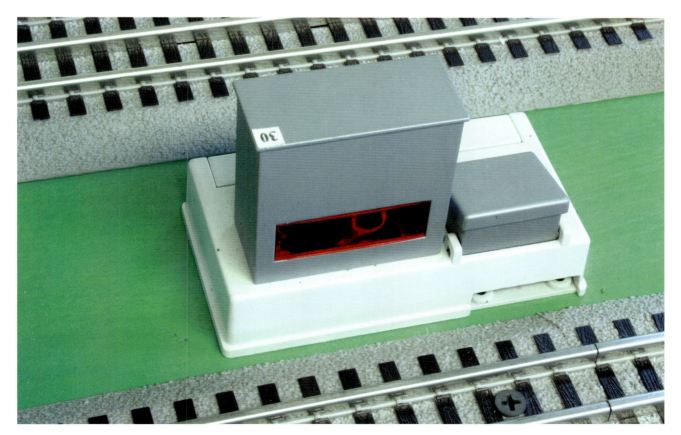

The 153IR Controller (6-14111) is an infrared light–emitting device that activates operating accessories with no change to the track.

CHAPTER 5

FasTrack on a 5x9 Ping-Pong Table

The incredible realism of Lionel's trains is breathtaking when you view the models from the same angles you would view a real train. Unfortunately, to watch these replicas close up and personal from the floor is awkward for all but six-year-olds. Elevating the tracks and trains to tabletop height is the solution. Realistic viewing is just one advantage of tabletop layout—tracks and trains on the floor collect more dirt and grime and are far more likely to be damaged with an accidental kick.

The Portable Table

The permanent and dedicated tabletop is certainly the ideal place to operate your Lionel FasTrack trains and accessories. There are examples of some of the best tabletop layouts in Chapter 10. You can, however, have just as much joy with a FasTrack layout on a portable table. The portable table can be as small as 4x6 feet, or you can use multiple tables (see Chapter 10) to fill a basement.

Self-storing Ping-Pong tables have a 2x5-foot platform with casters.

Two levels of action and three trains can operate in just 5x9 feet.

A variety of tables can make your Lionel layout as portable as the trains themselves. The 5x9 Ping-Pong table is an obvious choice because it is easy to find, sometimes even used. There are also portable styles of Ping-Pong tables that range from two plain 4 1/2x5 painted boards that you can place on a pool table or sawhorses, to simple 4 1/2x5 boards with card table–style folding legs, to clever fold-up tables with their own built-in wheeled storage platforms. I opted for the style shown in the photo, which folds upward to occupy just 2x5 feet of floor space. There's room inside the folded-up table halves to store boxes of track, buildings, and the felt and carpet antiskid mats I use for the scenery.

Most permanent Lionel layouts are built on tables sturdy enough to walk on. A Ping-Pong table is most certainly too weak to walk on—don't even think about it. However, if you place one 5-foot end against the wall you can walk around the remaining three sides and reach a derailed train anywhere on the layout.

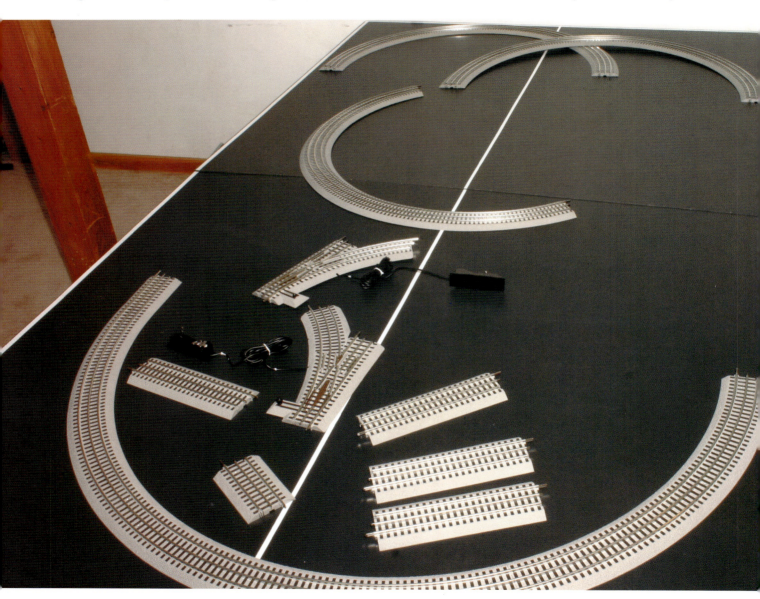

You can lay out the track for this plan or create your own. I assemble segments of curves to make the plan-as-you-go concept quicker.

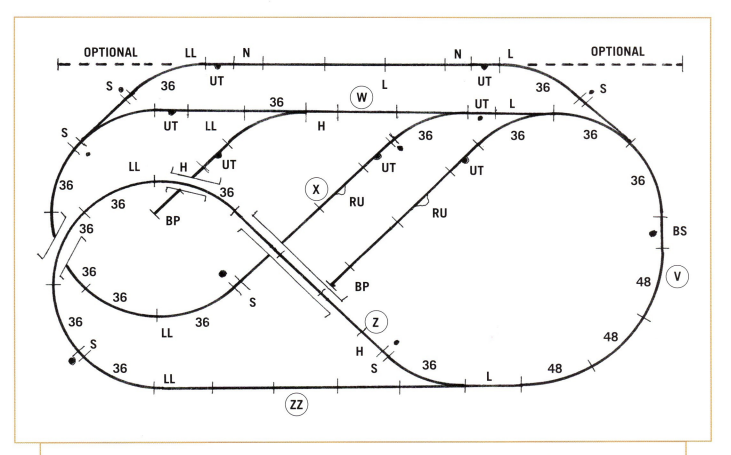

The Ping-Pong table layout with five electrically isolated blocks. The locations of the short insulated track sections are shown by the letter S. For this layout, the suggested places to connect the wires for the five blocks are identified as V, W, X, Z, and ZZ. This layout uses 036 curves and switches, except for the one 90-degree curve assembled from 048 track in the lower right. The layout can be extended in length by adding sets of straight track sections at all three places marked "L" or at the three places marked "LL."

FASTRACK SECTIONS REQUIRED:

Quantity	Symbol	Part No.	Description:
3	H	6-12024	Half-Straight Track
16	None	6-12014	10-inch Straight Track
2	BP	6-12059	Earthen Bumper
1	BS	6-12060	Block Section (insulated half-straight track)
2	N	6-12025	4 1/2-inch Straight Track
2	RU	6-12054	Operating Track
6	S	6102047350	1 3/8-inch Insulated Straight (furnished with 060 and 072 switches and as a replacement part; ballast shoulder on one side only)
7	UT	6-12020	Uncoupling Track
12	36	6-12015	036 45-Degree Curved Track
3	48	6-12043	048 30-Degree Curved Track
4	36	6-12045	036 Remote Switch (Left Hand)
2	36	6-12046	036 Remote Switch (Right Hand)

SPACE REQUIRED: 5x9 feet

A 5x18 Portable Layout

If you have more space, say 9x20 feet, you can put two Ping-Pong tables end to end for a 5x18 peninsula-style layout. That 9x20 feet is about half the size of most two-car garages. The extra 4 feet of width are needed for access aisles down the two long sides of the layout and the extra 2 feet of length is needed for an access aisle across one end of the layout. Frankly, 2 feet is tight, with no room for two people to pass in that aisle—3 feet is better. You can extend this plan (and most others, too) by simply adding pairs of standard 10-inch straights on opposite sides of the layout at the places marked "L" on the plan. You would need three 8-foot lengths of straight track (nine 6-12014 standard 10-inch Straight Tracks and one 6-12024 Half-Straight) in each of the three "L" locations to fill 5x18 feet with this track plan.

You could, of course, be a bit more creative when inserting the track sections. I suggest using four straights on each side of the two reversing loops at the points marked "LL" to lengthen them so they will hold longer trains in Blocks W, X, Z, and ZZ.

Operations on 5x9 Feet of Railroad

This plan is a loop-to-loop plan like those in Chapter 8, but with the two reversing loops placed one on top of the other. The second reversing loop is elevated 4 3/4 inches above the first on a set of 6-12038 Elevated Trestles and a 6-12772 Truss Bridge with Flashers and Piers supporting the upper-level track. One half of a set of 6-12037 Graduated Trestle Set bents supports the track as it climbs to the upper-level reverse loop.

Cover the bare table with antiskid mats for area rugs and a piece of 6x11-foot beige felt. Assemble all track to be sure it fits as planned.

The Graduated
Trestle Set
(6-12037),
Elevated
Trestle Set
(6-12038),
and any
bridges you
use can be
installed next.

Add some action
accessories and
enough buildings
to create a
small town.

The block wiring allowing two trains to operate on this layout is explained in Chapters 3 and 8, but a third train can be operated if one of the three is parked at the passing siding at the top of the plan.

The layout is even more fun to operate if you use locomotives equipped with Lionel TrainMaster Command Control and the layout is powered with the TrainMaster Command Control components explained in Chapter 3. The Lionel 1890-era 4-4-0 steam locomotive in the photo has not yet been made with TrainMaster, but you can substitute a number of small steam or diesel locomotives to pull a

TrainMaster-powered passenger train. The Burlington Northern GP9 has a custom paint scheme, but Lionel has offered this style of locomotive with TrainMaster Command Control. With TrainMaster, three trains can follow each other around the layout. You must time their paths, however, so that any passing takes place on the passing siding at the top of the layout.

There is ample opportunity for switching individual cars in and out of trains and in and out of the sidings. There are 6-12020 Uncoupling Tracks at both ends of the passing siding so a locomotive coming

The upper-level reverse loop is supported on an Elevated Trestle Set (6-12038) with a single truss bridge.

from either direction can uncouple from the train on either track. There are three more Uncoupling Tracks—one on each of three industrial sidings. Two of the three sidings also have 6-12054 Operating Tracks so you can use action cars like the milk car and cattle car, as well as the various log- and coal-dumping cars. On this layout, there's a 1950s-era Lionel coaling station (more recently sold as the 6-32921 Electric Coaling Station) located between two of the sidings and the unloading platform for an Automatic Refrigerated Milk Car.

There is enough space for a small town and a country scene on this layout. The small town items include:

- 6-49812 – #755 Talking Station
- 6-24190 – Station Platforms (three)
- 6-14086 – #38 Operating Water Tower
- 6-34121 – Bungalow
- 6-34108 – Suburban House
- 6-34113 – Large Suburban House II
- 6-14091 – Automatic Gateman
- 6-12036 – Grade Crossing
- 6-12052 – Grade Crossing with Flashers

The cars and trucks are die-cast models from Corgi and other toy makers. The roads are simple strips of gray cardboard with smudges of powdered black pencil lead.

The houses are from the Lionelville series. The streets are cardboard.

Portable Scenery

Felt cloth is a good choice for portable scenery because it has the texture of grass with no loose fibers to cause electrical problems. First, cover the table with antiskid mats sold for area rugs. This will help hold the felt in place and quiet the trains.

Green, beige, and white felt is available in 6-foot widths at most sewing shops. Use the green for summer, the beige for winter or arid scenes, and the white, of course, for snow scenes. If you want to disable the layout to store it, disassemble the track, put the structures in boxes, and roll up the felt.

Buy about 20 percent more felt than the length and width of your layout to leave enough material to be bulged upward by wads of newspaper to create mountains. If, for example, you are covering a 5x9-foot layout, use about 6x11 feet of felt. Any excess can be tucked under the edges on the floor or thumbtacked to the underside of the tabletop.

You can improve the realism of the light beige felt by adding splotches of grass-green latex paint. Lay the felt on the floor and use a roller to dab the paint in patches. If you choose green felt for a summer look, apply splotches of earth-brown latex paint

A small strip of Mountains-in-Minutes Flexrock strata lies beneath a mountain of Life-Like trees in the country portion of the layout.

The Lionel bridge abutments are about 1/2 inch higher than the Elevated Trestle bents to create the highest altitude on the layout.

The Automatic Gateman, Electric Coaling Station, and Operating Water Tower are, perhaps, the most classic Lionel action accessories.

to create the effect of patches of bare earth among the grass and weeds. Wad up some newspapers and tuck them beneath the felt to produce hills. Keep the hills or mountains a couple of inches away from the track so they don't tilt up the track and cause derailments.

Faller (170791), Kibri (4126), and Noch (60850 and 60851) are three choices of clear plastic "water" sheets that your dealer should be able to order for you. Or, you can simply crumple up aluminum foil and flatten it to get a similar effect. Cut the rippled clear plastic to the shape of the river or lake you desire and just lay it on the felt. If you need a longer river, use a second piece of the rippled plastic and hide the joint with a bridge.

Your Lionel dealer should also be able to supply a foliage material called lichen, a Norwegian moss that

The passenger train waits on the straight leg of the lower reverse loop for the freight to complete its trip downgrade to the passing siding.

The station area includes a #755 Talking Station (6-49812) and three Station Platforms (6-24190).

has been softened in glycerin and dyed green. Shake off any loose bits and place the lichen right on the grass mat to simulate bushes. Cover the edges of the rivers or lakes with lichen to provide a more realistic shoreline.

Your Lionel dealer can also order a wide range of ready-to-install trees. The trees on this layout are the Life-Like 1971 Giant Oak Trees with some Faller 181363 Elm, 181364 Beech, and 181463 Chestnut

trees that are available to dealers through Walthers.

Lightweight flexible foam rubber rocks are available from Mountains-in-Minutes. These 7x16-inch Flexrocks are available in three textures: 501 Rock Canyon, 502 Rock Embankment, and 503 Rock Gorge. Bend the foam rubber rocks to fit around the tracks and attach them to the felt with safety pins. The textures and colors are as realistic as real rocks.

CHAPTER 6

Planning Your Layout

Every model railroad begins with a single section of track and expands from there. Lionel makes it easier to assemble and to operate a complete model railroad than any other model railroad system. All Lionel locomotives, rolling stock, accessories, and track are ready-to-use. And FasTrack makes track-laying literally, and audibly, a "snap."

Creating Your Own Empire

The FasTrack line features a wide selection of curved track diameters and different lengths of straight track, switches, and even snap-in elevated trestle sets. The selection of curved tracks begins with a standard 36-inch-diameter circle and ranges, in 12-inch increments, to 48-, 60-, 72-, and 84-inch-diameter curves (which Lionel refers to as simply 036, 048, 060, 072, and 084) for really massive model railroads. Lionel has always measured the size of a curve by the diameter of the circle that the curve creates at the outside rail. Because the outer ends of the ties and the ballast

Lionel's massive F3A and F3B diesels and extruded-metal passenger cars look best on 060 or larger curves.

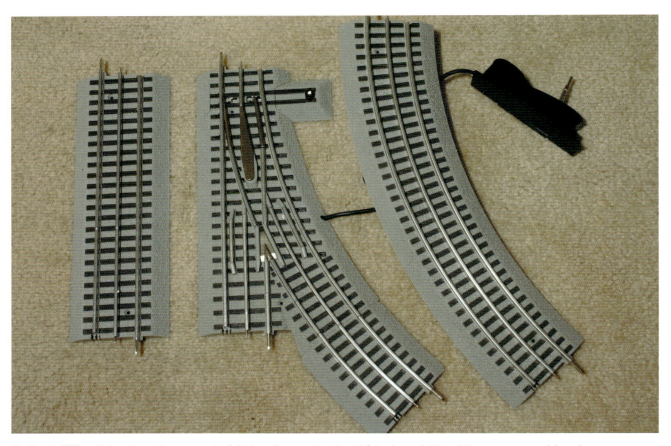

FasTrack 036 switches have the same straight length as a standard 10-inch straight and the same curved length as a full-length 036 curve track section.

require a few more inches, you actually cannot squeeze a 180-degree 036 (36-inch) curve onto a 3-foot tabletop or a 180-degree 084 (84-inch) curve on a 7-foot wide tabletop.

The standard FasTrack 036 curve is just a bit larger than the traditional 27-inch all-metal track curve (O-27 track) and the 31-inch (O-31) all-metal curve, but the geometry is the same and the 10-inch FasTrack straight matches that of the traditional O-31 straight track sections. You can, then, use track plans for the smallest traditional O-27 and O-31 track with FasTrack, but the layout will require a few more inches of width and length to accommodate the slightly larger curves.

The 12-inch difference in curve diameters was a deliberate and clever part of FasTrack design. The 6 inches between curves means even the longest locomotives and cars will not sideswipe one another. The

036, 060, 072, and 084 curves are all based on quarter-circles, halves of quarter circles, and quarters of quarter circles, or 45 degrees, 22 1/2 degrees, and 11 1/4 degrees, respectively.

For reasons unknown, the 48-inch curves are based on 30 degrees of a circle, so it takes 12 of them to make a full circle and they only align with other curves when the curve is 90, 180, or 270 degrees around. And there are no 48-inch switches. The 48-inch (048) curves are useful, however, for assembling double-track ovals with an 036 inside oval and an 048 outside oval, or for a layout with an 060 outside oval and an 048 inside oval.

The 084 curves are useful for larger layouts because they can be used as the outer oval for a set of 072 and 084 ovals on a double-track main line like the one shown in Chapter 7. Chapter 9 explains more about the geometry of the system.

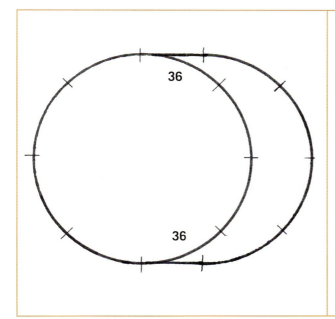

Add a pair of 036 switches and two pieces of 036 curve to make this layout with a passing siding.

FASTRACK SECTIONS REQUIRED:

Quantity	Symbol	Part No.	Description
10	None	6-12015	036 45-Degree Curved Track
1	36	6-12017	036 Manual Switch (Left Hand)
1	36	6-12018	036 Manual Switch (Right Hand)
or:			
1	36	6-12045	036 Remote Switch (Left Hand)
1	36	6-12046	036 Remote Switch (Right Hand)

SPACE REQUIRED: 3 1/2x4 1/2 feet

Simple Substitution to Expand a Layout

FasTrack is designed to make it simple to add switches and create passing sidings, multitrack yards, and even double-track main lines.

All FasTrack switches include separate short sections of track. The 036 switch has one removable 1/4-length curve that allows the curved route of the 036 switch to exactly match the length of the standard 036 curve so you can use the switch as-is to replace any full-length 036 curve. The straight length on the 036 switch is the same 10 inches as standard straight so you can replace any standard straight with an 036 switch.

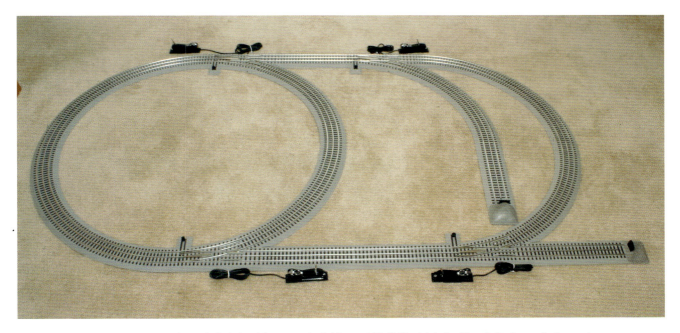

This compact plan could be enlarged slightly with more straights and Half-Straights to fill a 4x8 piece of plywood.

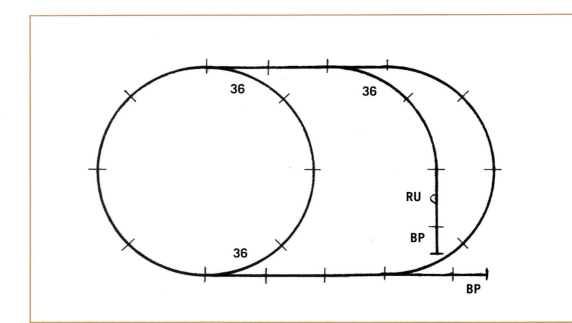

Two more 036 switches and some straight track sections add more running room and two industrial sidings to the basic oval and passing track layout in Fig. 6-1.

FASTRACK SECTIONS REQUIRED:

Quantity	Symbol	Part No.	Description
2	BP	6-12035	Lighted Bumper
or			
	BP	6-12059	Earthen Bumper
1	RU	6-12054	Operating Track
3	None	6-12014	10-inch Straight Track
9	None	6-12015	036 45-Degree Curved Track
1	36	6-12017	036 Manual Switch (Left Hand)
1	36	6-12018	036 Manual Switch (Right Hand)
or:			
1	36	6-12045	036 Remote Switch (Left Hand)
1	36	6-12046	036 Remote Switch (Right Hand)

SPACE REQUIRED: 3 1/2x6 feet

You can start with a simple oval and add a pair of switches and a matching set of curved tracks to complete a second half-loop. Lionel offers a FasTrack 6-12028 Inner Passing Loop Add-on Track Pack that includes enough track to add a simple passing siding inside an 036 oval.

To further expand that basic oval with passing siding, add a stub-ended industrial siding with a right-hand 036 switch at the top of the oval. I expanded the oval a bit by adding a piece of straight track at the top and two more straights at the bottom. Add a second stub-ended industrial siding by replacing one of the end curves with a left-hand 036 switch. This add-and-substitute system makes it possible to expand your Lionel FasTrack layout into any size or shape for the space you have available—and you can do it with just a couple of track sections at a time.

The Variety of Versatile Switches

With the exception of the FasTrack wye switch, which has routes leading both left and right, all FasTrack switches are available as either left or right (a right-hand switch has the curved diverging route leading off to the right).

Lionel's 036, 060, and 072 switches are each designed to produce 6-inch center-to-center track spacing when used to make crossovers on double-track main line, enough to keep the longest car and locomotives from sideswiping one another through curves. By removing the two short curves from the 036 switches, you can use two right-hand or two left-hand 036 switches to make a crossover with the same 6-inch center-to-center spacing that is possible with 060 and 072 switches. There are several double-track main line plans for curves from 36 to 84 inches in Chapter 7.

The 060 and 072 switches include a third piece of short straight track with no ballast shoulders on either side that is designed to be placed between a set of right-hand or left-hand 060 or 072 switches to create a crossover with 6-inch center-to-center track spacing. The short sections with a single ballast shoulder must be removed from the curved side of both switches to allow just that third short section to be installed. Lionel offers these short straights as service parts if you do not have any left over from 060, 072, or wye switches. The short straight track section with no ballast shoulders is number 6102047150 and the short straight with a single ballast shoulder is number 6102047350 and both can be ordered by your Lionel dealer. The short straights are marked "S" on the plans. In some cases you can substitute the slightly longer (6-12026) 1 3/4-inch straight, which is identified as "SS" on the plans.

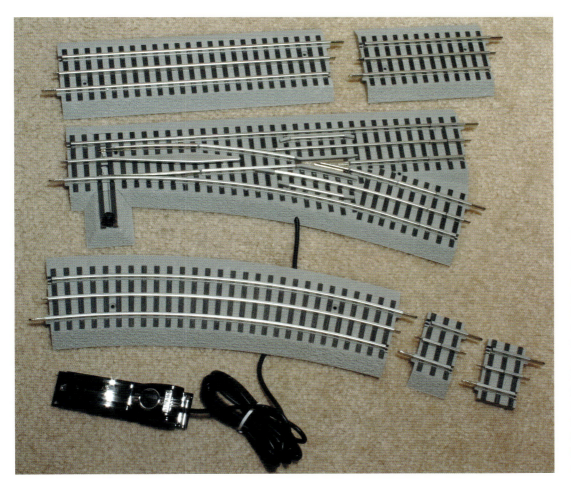

Lionel 060 switches are the length of a full standard straight plus a Half-Straight. The curved side matches an 060 curve plus the length of two pieces of short straights. The switches are furnished with three pieces of short straight track.

The 060 FasTrack switches are a rather odd size because they are too small for the largest locomotives. A few of Lionel's medium-size locomotives are designed with 60 inches as a minimum curve size. The 060 switches are, however, far more realistic than the 036 switches and I recommend using them on smaller layouts just for their appearance. The on-the-floor layout in Chapter 11 was assembled with 060 rather than 036 track strictly because the larger curves look more realistic, especially with longer locomotives and passenger cars. The 060 switches are 1 1/2-inch standard straight track sections (15 inches) long (plus the length of the 1 3/8-inch-long removable section). The curved length is the same as an 060 curve; however, there is an extra 1 3/8-inch straight piece snapped onto the end. That piece is necessary to clear the ballast shoulder for the adjoining piece of track. If you are willing to saw off a small corner of the ballast shoulder on the adjoining piece of track, you can eliminate the short pieces and squeeze in more track if necessary. Those 1 3/8-inch-long pieces are useful, however, in providing insulating track sections for operating two or more trains if the wires on the bottom of the short straight are unplugged, as described in Chapter 3.

The 072 curves are necessary for many of the largest Lionel locomotives designed to operate on a 72-inch minimum diameter curve. If you want to operate any locomotive Lionel makes, you need to use only 072 switches and either 072 or 084 curves because the largest locomotives will derail on 036, 048, or even 060 curves. The curved length of the 072 switch is the same as the standard 072 curve plus that 1 3/8-inch removable straight. The straight length of the 072 switch is an unusual 15 3/4 inches. You can, however, match that length with a standard 10-inch FasTrack Straight Track (6-12014) plus the 4 1/2-inch FasTrack Straight Track (6-12025) plus one of the short 1 3/8-inch straights from the 060 or 072 switches.

The FasTrack 6-12047 072 Wye Remote Switch has 72-inch-diameter curved routes leading both left and right for an equal distance. The switch itself is 12 inches long, equal to a half of an 072 11 1/4-Degree Half-Curved Track (6-12055) plus a Half-Straight Track (6-12024), which is 5 inches long, plus a short (1 3/8-inch) piece of insulated track on each route. It is difficult to include a wye switch in a conventional track plan, but there are examples in the double-loop plan in Chapter 8. On a real railroad it is not uncommon for three wye switches to be combined to create a reversing track section that is also called a wye, like the example in Chapter 6 (which is also incorporated in the layout in Chapter 10).

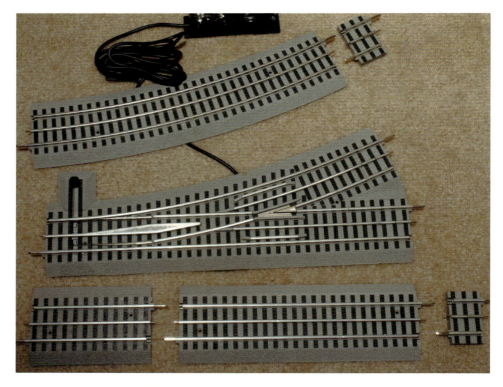

Lionel 072 switches are 15 3/4 inches long on the straight route with the curved side matching an 072 full-length curve plus a short straight. The 072 switches are also furnished with three pieces of short straight track.

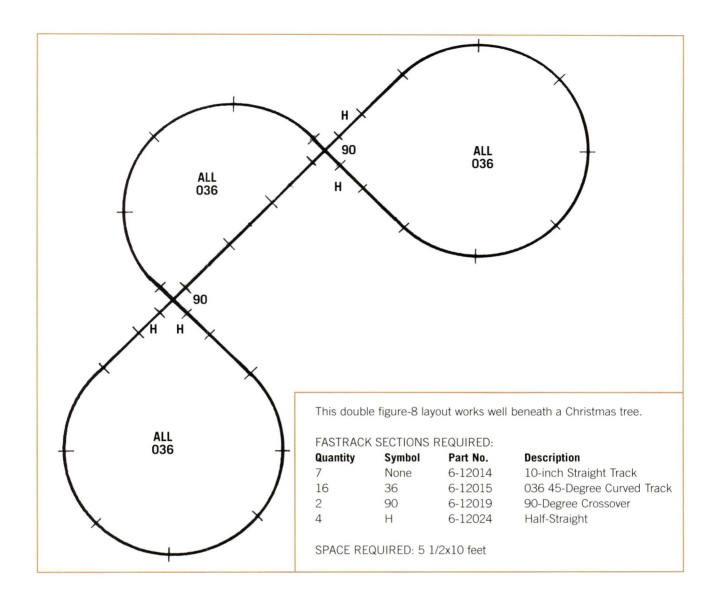

This double figure-8 layout works well beneath a Christmas tree.

FASTRACK SECTIONS REQUIRED:

Quantity	Symbol	Part No.	Description
7	None	6-12014	10-inch Straight Track
16	36	6-12015	036 45-Degree Curved Track
2	90	6-12019	90-Degree Crossover
4	H	6-12024	Half-Straight

SPACE REQUIRED: 5 1/2x10 feet

Double-Crossing Figure-8 Layouts

The Lionel layout with track arranged to form a figure 8 is one of the most exciting layouts. The sight of the train crossing another track, perhaps almost catching its own caboose or observation car in the process, is a delight. The FasTrack system is designed to make figure-8 plans possible for all sizes of curves in the system. There are plans for these layouts using 036 and 060 curves here, and a plan with 072 curves in Chapter 11.

If a single figure 8 is exciting, a double-crossing 8 is even more so. I find these plans to be particularly applicable to around-the-tree layouts at Christmas time. The tree goes in one loop, leaving two crossings and two loops visible in front of or beside the tree. The plans can also be enlarged to create L-shaped layouts with, perhaps, additional switches for passing sidings.

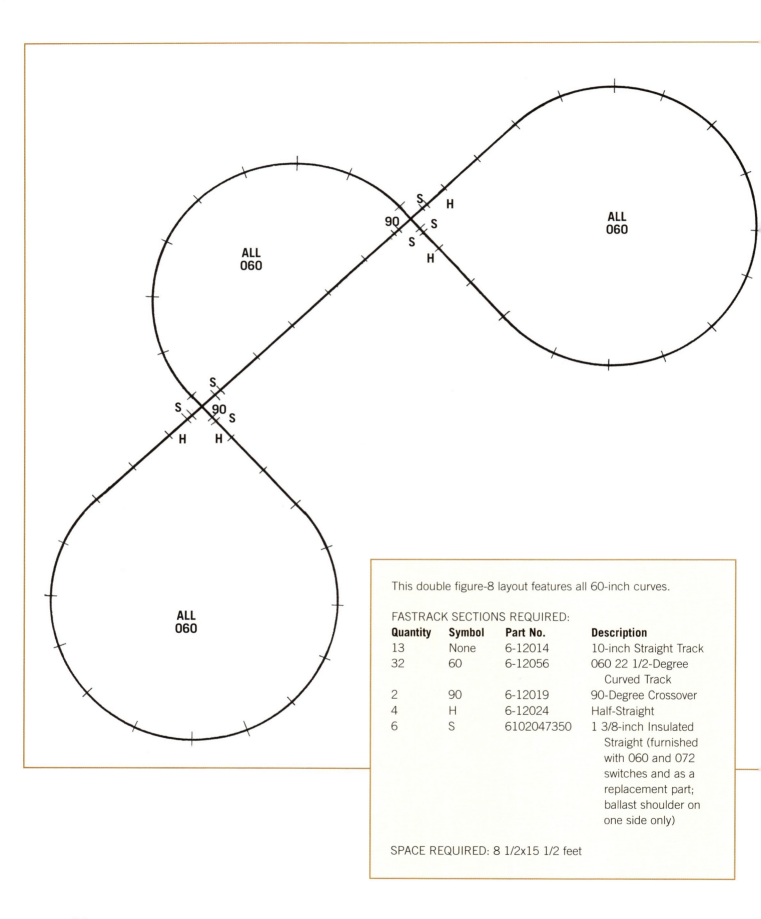

ALL
060

ALL
060

ALL
060

This double figure-8 layout features all 60-inch curves.

FASTRACK SECTIONS REQUIRED:

Quantity	Symbol	Part No.	Description
13	None	6-12014	10-inch Straight Track
32	60	6-12056	060 22 1/2-Degree Curved Track
2	90	6-12019	90-Degree Crossover
4	H	6-12024	Half-Straight
6	S	6102047350	1 3/8-inch Insulated Straight (furnished with 060 and 072 switches and as a replacement part; ballast shoulder on one side only)

SPACE REQUIRED: 8 1/2x15 1/2 feet

The Inverted Figure 8

The inverted 8 is another variation in track design that makes an interesting layout to watch as the train travels what looks like a double-track main line. The plan included here is for 036 and 048 curves, but the layout can be assembled with larger curves like the figure-8 layouts in this chapter. The inverted 8 can be assembled with 060 and 072 curves or with 072 and 084 curves.

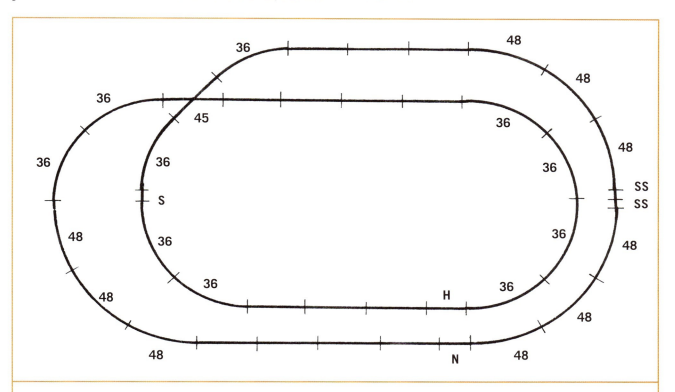

This inverted figure-8 layout can be assembled on one level as shown. If you remove the 45-degree crossing and replace it with two pieces of standard 10-inch Straight Track (6-12014), you can elevate the tracks so the inner oval crosses above the outer oval. Support the tracks as they climb up and down the grade with the 22 bents in the Graduated Trestle Set (6-12037) and a long bridge like the Lionel Truss Bridge with Flasher and Piers (6-12772).

FASTRACK SECTIONS REQUIRED:

Quantity	Symbol	Part No.	Description
14*	None	6-12014	10-inch Straight Track
10	36	6-12015	036 45-Degree Curved Track
9	48	6-12043	048 30-Degree Curved Track
1	H	6-12024	Half-Straight
1	N	6-12025	4 1/2-inch Straight Track
2	S	6102047350	1 3/8-inch Insulated Straight (furnished with 060 and 072 switches and as a replacement part; ballast shoulder on one side only)
1	SS	6-12026	1 3/4-inch Straight Track
1*	45	6-12051	45-Degree Crossover

*Note: Use 16 standard straights (6-12014) and eliminate the 45-Degree Crossover (6-12051) for an over-and-under layout.

SPACE REQUIRED: 5x8 1/2 feet

Climbing the Grade

Lionel locomotives have ample power to pull trains up grades. The up and down hill portions of the layout add a third dimension that is visually more interesting than a flat layout. The sight of one train passing over another is, perhaps, the most exciting scene in railroading and you can recreate it on your Lionel layout.

The Lionel FasTrack Graduated Trestle Set (6-12037) includes enough trestle bents to raise the track 5 1/2 inches above the tabletop. (The system is illustrated in Chapter 5.) The 11 bents require about 110 inches to allow the track to climb the grade to the top and another 110 inches to allow the track to descend back to the tabletop. That's roughly 11 sections of track for the uphill grade and another 11 sections for the downhill grade, so you will need a layout with at least 22 sections of track on either side of the bridge area where one track passes above the other.

You can convert most of the figure-8 plans into over-and-under layouts by replacing the level 90-degree or 45-degree crossovers with an elevated track. The inverted oval plan has enough track length so you can replace the level 45-degree crossing with a Graduated Trestle Set. Plus, there is another 3 feet or so of track to leave room for a long bridge like the 6-12772 Truss Bridge with Flasher and Piers to span the lower track. Locate the bridge on the straight portion of the track so the uphill grade begins on the outer oval (running clockwise) to climb up the hill, then comes back down on the inner oval. The layout in Chapter 5 has an overpass, as do some of the layouts in Chapter 8.

The upper-level track for an inverted figure-8 layout can be supported on a Graduated Trestle Set (6-12037) like that used on this 072 double-loop layout also featured in Chapter 8.

CHAPTER 7

Double-Track Layouts for Two Trains

Most Class 1 railroads operate a main line with two parallel tracks, one for eastbound trains and the other for westbound trains. The trains can operate continuously with little chance of head-on collisions. They can also operate efficiently, with a stop at a siding only necessary if a slower train is passed by a faster train.

That continuous operation of trains traveling in opposite directions is something that can be easily recreated with FasTrack. The simplest way to run two trains is to simply set up two independent ovals. The ovals can be as small as 4 1/2x7 1/2 feet with 036 and 048 ovals or massive 10x24-foot ovals of 072 curves like Peter Perry's layout in Chapter 10.

Double-Track Main Line Crossovers

If you want to vary the scene, however, one option is to allow the trains to swap over from the inside oval to the outside oval. To do that, you will need what the real railroads call a crossover. Lionel calls them 45-Degree and 90-Degree Crossovers, as well.

Even a small layout on the floor can be designed to operate two trains, like this 6 1/2x8-foot layout adapted from the 1939 Coal Field Railroad in Chapter 11.

You really need two right- and two left-hand switches so the trains can cross over from one oval to the other without the need to back up. The electrically isolated blocks (A, B, C and D on the plans) and the electrical wiring needed to accomplish this are described in Chapter 2. If you use TrainMaster Command Control locomotives and power supplies you won't need the electrically isolated blocks.

Expanding the Double-Track Main Line

The simple double-track oval plans described in this book are designed to be the basic building blocks for a larger railroad. You can add just a few straights or you can bend and expand the plans to fill your available space. You can also incorporate the reverse loops and yards in Chapter 12. Two of the really massive layouts in Chapter 11 feature double-track main lines, one an oval and the other a reverse loop-to-reverse-loop layout.

A double-track oval with 036 and 048 curves and 036 switches. A similar plan, with 060 switches, is in Chapter 3. The letters A, B, C, and D are where wires would connect for four electrically isolated blocks, as described in Chapter 3.

FASTRACK SECTIONS REQUIRED:

Quantity	Symbol	Part No.	Description
8	None	6-12014	10-inch Straight Track
8	S	6102047350	1 3/8-inch Insulated Straight (furnished with 060 and 072 switches and as a replacement part; ballast shoulder on one side only)
8	36	6-12015	036 45-Degree Curved Track
2	36	6-12045	036 Remote Switch (Left Hand)
2	36	6-12046	036 Remote Switch (Right Hand)
12	48	6-12043	048 30-Degree Curved Track

SPACE REQUIRED: 4 1/2x7 1/2 feet

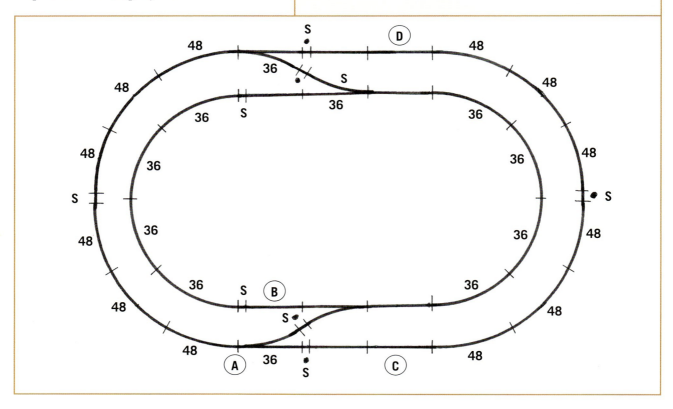

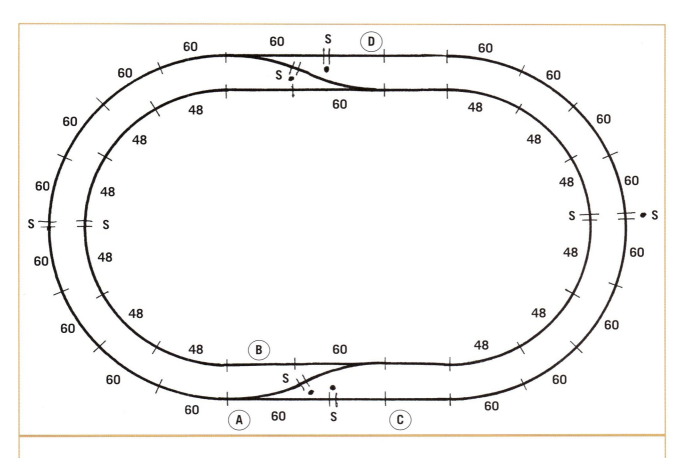

BA double-track oval with 048 and 060 curves and 060 switches. The letters A, B, C, and D are where wires connect for four electrically isolated blocks, as described in Chapter 3.

FASTRACK SECTIONS REQUIRED:

Quantity	Symbol	Part No.	Description
8	None	6-12014	10-inch Straight Track
8	S	6102047350	1 3/8-inch Insulated Straight (furnished with 060 switches and as a replacement part; ballast shoulder on one side only)
2	60	6-12057	060 Remote Switch (Left Hand)
2	60	6-12058	060 Remote Switch (Right Hand)
12	48	6-12043	048 30-Degree Curved Track
16	60	6-12056	060 221/2-Degree Curved Track

SPACE REQUIRED: 5 1/2x8 1/2 feet

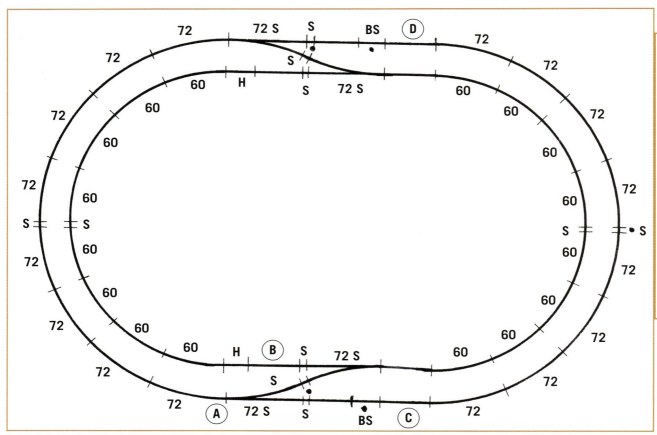

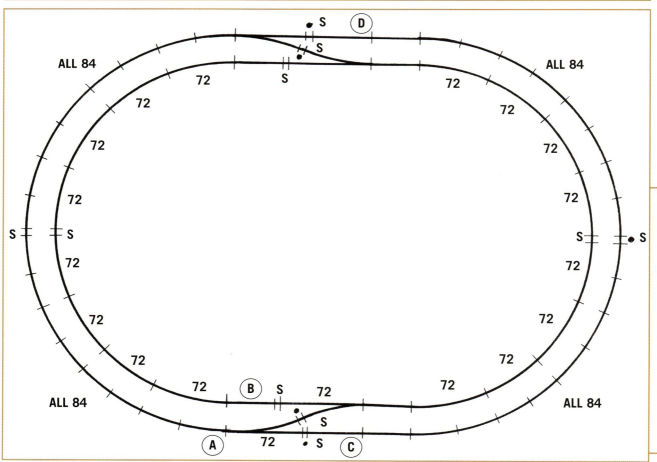

A double-track oval with 060 and 072 curves and 072 switches. The letters A, B, C, and D are where wires connect for four electrically isolated blocks as described in Chapter 3.

FASTRACK SECTIONS REQUIRED:

Quantity	Symbol	Part No.	Description
8	None	6-12014	10-inch Straight Track
2	H	6-12024	Half-Straight
2	BS	6-12060	Block Section (insulated track)
8	S	6102047350	1 3/8-inch Insulated Straight (furnished with 072 switches and as a replacement part; ballast shoulder on one side only)
2	72	6-12048	072 Remote Switch (Left Hand)
2	72	6-12049	072 Remote Switch (Right Hand)
16	60	6-12056	060 22 1/2-Degree Curved Track
16	72	6-12041	072 22 1/2-Degree Curved Track

SPACE REQUIRED: 6 1/2x10 feet

Peter Perry arranged the track on his layout to create five completely separate loops so five trains run at once, each with its own transformer.

A double-track oval with 072 and 084 curves and 072 switches. Since the 072 curves are the smallest size used on this layout, even the largest Lionel locomotives can operate on the inner and outer ovals. The letters A, B, C, and D are where wires connect for four electrically isolated blocks as described in Chapter 3.

FASTRACK SECTIONS REQUIRED:

Quantity	Symbol	Part No.	Description
8	None	6-12014	10-inch Straight Track
8	S	6102047350	1 3/8-inch Insulated Straight (furnished with 072 switches and as a replacement part; ballast shoulder on one side only)
2	72	6-12048	072 Remote Switch (Left Hand)
2	72	6-12049	072 Remote Switch (Right Hand)
16	72	6-12041	072 22 1/2-Degree Curved Track
32	84	6-12061	084 11 1/4-Degree Curved Track

SPACE REQUIRED: 7 1/2x11feet

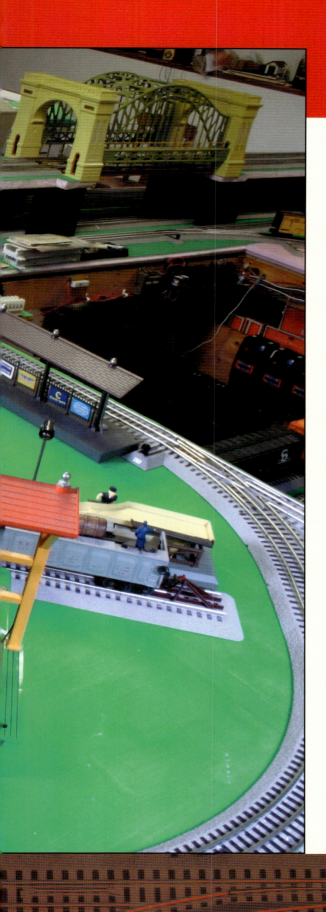

Layouts to Allow Reversing Trains

Of course trains are supposed to run eastbound as well as westbound because that's how most real railroads designate their train movements. The question is, where (and when) do they change direction? On a real railroad trains usually change from eastbound to westbound only when they reach their final destinations. A westbound Chicago–Omaha train might terminate in Omaha and either be completely rearranged in the multitrack freight or passenger yard or the locomotive and crew assigned to another train heading eastbound.

On our model railroads, there is seldom the space for a massive yard, especially not two yards for both east and west terminals. Still, we want be able to run trains in both directions without the need to hand-carry the locomotive from one end of the train the other. You can arrange the track so it automatically changes the train's direction. The most common

Bill Langsdorf included a reverse loop on the upper-level track of his two-level layout featured in Chapter 10.

A freight train waits on the lower reversing loop of the 9x12-foot layout while the passenger train negotiates the upper-level loop and heads out on the mainline.

track arrangement is called a reversing loop because that's just what this loop of track accomplishes. Model railroaders tend to design layouts that run from one reversing loop down a main line to a second reversing loop. This way, trains can travel from, say, Town P in reverse loop P to Town Q in reverse loop Q, then back again without ever being moved by hand. You'll see examples of compact layouts with reverse loops in this chapter and some larger examples in Chapters 11 and 12.

Loop-to-Loop Operations

Each of these loop-to-loop layouts has each of the two reverse loops divided into two blocks. Chapter 3 explains the need for these electrically isolating blocks and their wiring. The photo shows the wires, with large yellow dots on the center rail to indicate where the insulating track sections are needed. These

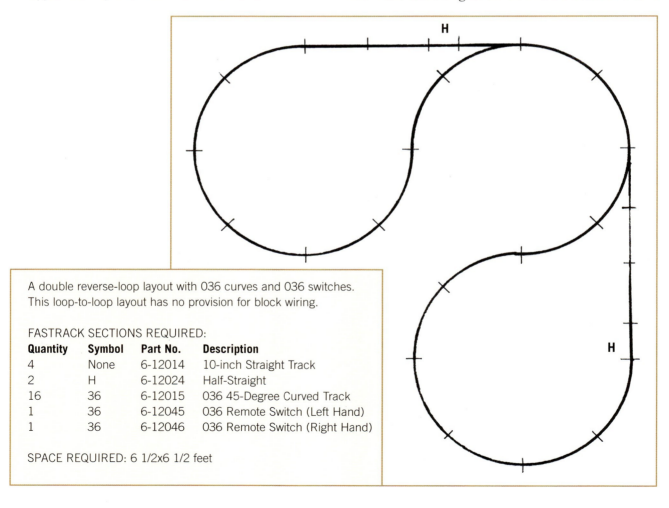

A double reverse-loop layout with 036 curves and 036 switches. This loop-to-loop layout has no provision for block wiring.

FASTRACK SECTIONS REQUIRED:

Quantity	Symbol	Part No.	Description
4	None	6-12014	10-inch Straight Track
2	H	6-12024	Half-Straight
16	36	6-12015	036 45-Degree Curved Track
1	36	6-12045	036 Remote Switch (Left Hand)
1	36	6-12046	036 Remote Switch (Right Hand)

SPACE REQUIRED: 6 1/2x6 1/2 feet

This simple reverse-loop-to-reverse-loop layout is the basis for some of the most interesting model railroads imaginable.

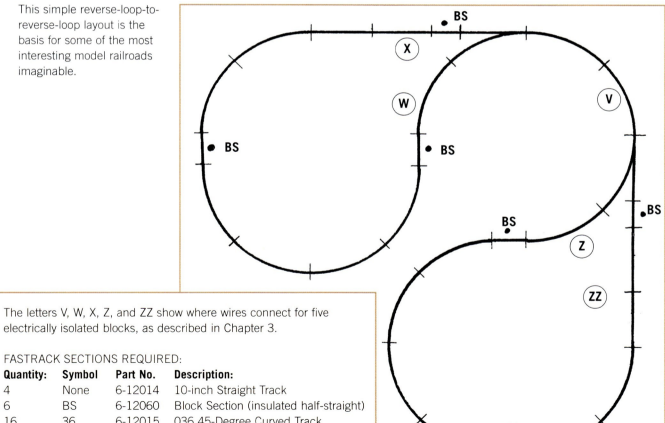

The letters V, W, X, Z, and ZZ show where wires connect for five electrically isolated blocks, as described in Chapter 3.

FASTRACK SECTIONS REQUIRED:

Quantity:	Symbol	Part No.	Description:
4	None	6-12014	10-inch Straight Track
6	BS	6-12060	Block Section (insulated half-straight)
16	36	6-12015	036 45-Degree Curved Track
1	36	6-12045	036 Remote Switch (Left Hand)
1	36	6-12046	036 Remote Switch (Right Hand)

SPACE REQUIRED: 6 1/2x6 1/2 feet

The addition of six Block Sections (6-12060), marked BS on the plans, divides the layout into four blocks (the shorter insulated track sections from the 060 and 072 switches could also have been used as described in Chapter 3). Four on-off switches provide power from the main block (just in front of the transformer) to each of the other three blocks. The fourth on-off switch (not shown) connects track along the rear wall.

loop-to-loop layouts require five blocks: two for each of the reverse loops and one for the main line. Since only one train will operate at any one time, one transformer is enough for the loop-to-loop layout. If the layout is large enough, you can add more main line blocks and a second transformer so two trains can operate at once. With TrainMaster Command Control locomotives and power supplies, you can operate two or more trains without the need for blocks.

Operations on Reverse Loop Layouts

Operations can start with Train 1 parked just short of the switch (turnout) at either of the tracks that exit out of upper-level reverse loop. When Train 2 enters the upper level reverse loop it runs almost all the way around and stops just behind Train 1. The block that controls that half of the reverse loop is then turned off so Train 2 can stop and park. The block beneath Train 1 can then be turned on and Train 1 can proceed out of the reverse loop and back on the main line heading for the second reversing loop. Train 2

can then be moved to the block previously occupied by Train 1. When Train 1 completes its travel around the layout it pulls up behind Train 2 and the whole sequence can be repeated.

These plans are really just large enough for two trains. Larger layouts can operate a third train, even with a single power pack. Since there is a reverse loop at both ends of this loop-to-loop layout, a third train (Train 3) can be parked in the second "half"—the lower reverse loop—to await the arrival of Train 1 behind Train 3. Train 3 can then proceed onto the main line and park behind Train 2. This musical chairs sequence of running just one train at a time while the other two are parked can be repeated indefinitely with the three trains.

A Room-Size Loop-to-Loop Layout

There's a delightful attic-based model railroad on page 29 of both *The Lionel Train Book* and *The Big Book of Lionel* that was reprinted from *The Model Builder's Handbook*. It's an example of how you can

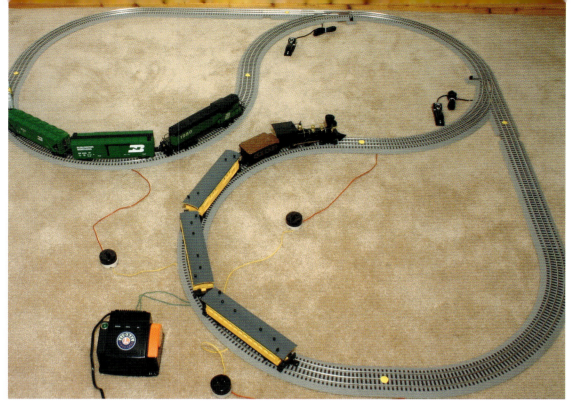

A train can be parked on either half of either reverse loop while the transformer operates the second train. With five blocks, it's possible to park a third train; the three would follow each other around the layout from block to block, musical-chairs style.

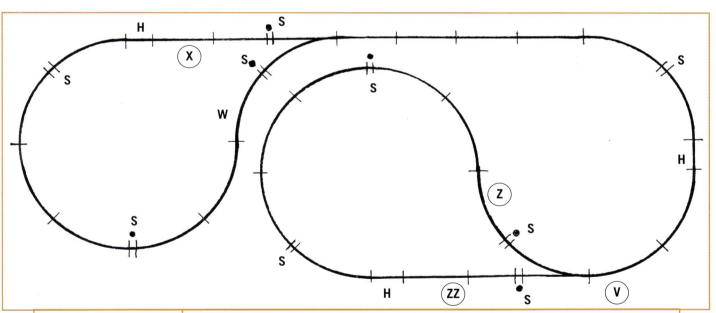

The main line on the reverse-loop-to-reverse-loop layout can be extended to fold the loops inside one another. The letters V, W, X, Z, and ZZ are where wires connect for five electrically isolated blocks as described in Chapter 3.

FASTRACK SECTIONS REQUIRED:

Quantity	Symbol	Part No.	Description
8	None	6-12014	10-inch Straight Track
3	H	6-12024	Half-Straight
9	S	6102047350	1 3/8-inch Insulated Straight (furnished with 060 and 072 switches and as a replacement part; ballast shoulder on one side only)
18	36	6-12015	036 45-Degree Curved Track
1	36	6-12045	036 Remote Switch (Left Hand)
1	36	6-12046	036 Remote Switch (Right Hand)

SPACE REQUIRED: 4x10 feet

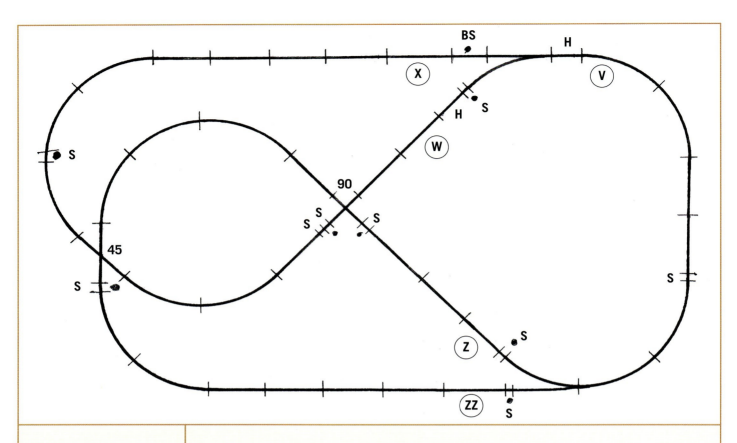

The main line on the reverse-loop-to-reverse-loop layout can be folded over itself on just one level with two crossings. The letters V, W, X, Z, and ZZ are where wires connect for five electrically isolated blocks, as described in Chapter 3.

FASTRACK SECTIONS REQUIRED:

Quantity	Symbol	Part No.	Description
19	None	6-12014	10-inch Straight Track
1	BS	6-12060	Block Section (insulated half-straight)
2	H	6-12024	Half-Straight
9	S	6102047	350 1 3/8-inch Insulated Straight (furnished with 060 and 072 switches and as a replacement part; ballast shoulder on one side only)
14	36	6-12015	036 45-Degree Curved Track
1	36	6-12045	036 Remote Switch (Left Hand)
1	36	6-12046	036 Remote Switch (Right Hand)
1	45	6-12051	45-Degree Crossover
1	90	6-12019	90-Degree Crossover

SPACE REQUIRED: 5 1/2x9 1/2 feet

expand a simple two-loop layout like those in this chapter into a massive 14x18-foot attic or basement empire with a double-track main line and four reverse loops. Each of the reverse loops is really just one of four destination cities for the trains. Loop A might be designated "Seattle," Loop B "Los Angeles," Loop C "Philadelphia," and Loop D "Miami," or, more realistically, some other destinations within the same or adjacent states. Real railroads often have routes in four or more directions and this layout can simulate them all.

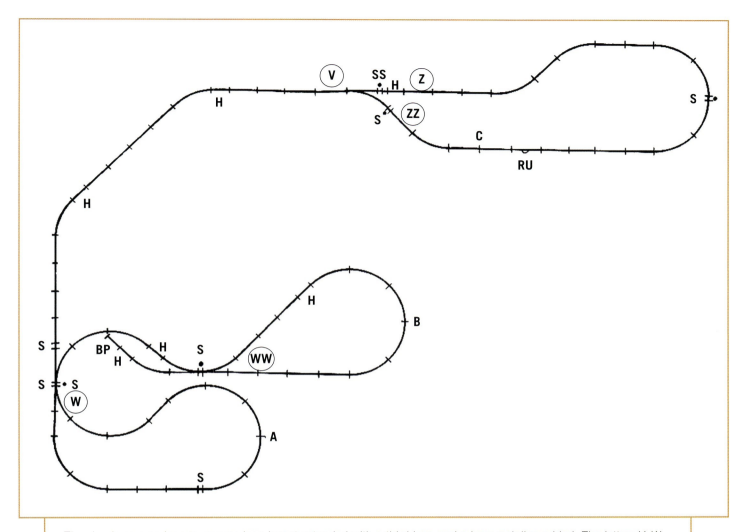

The simple reverse loop-to-reverse loop layout extended with a third loop and a long mainline added. The letters V, W, WW, Z, and ZZ are where wires would connect for five electrically isolated blocks, as described in Chapter 3.

FASTRACK SECTIONS REQUIRED:

Quantity	Symbol	Part No.	Description
36*	None	6-12014	10-inch Straight Track
1	BP	6-12035	Lighted Bumper
or:			
1	BP	6-12059	Earthen Bumper
6	H	6-12024	Half-Straight
1	RU	6-12054	Operating Track
8	S	6102047	350 1 3/8-inch Insulated Straight (furnished with 060 and 072 switches and as a replacement part; ballast shoulder on one side only)
26	36	6-12015	036 45-Degree Curved Track
2	36	6-12045	036 Remote Switch (Left Hand)
3	36	6-12046	036 Remote Switch (Right Hand)

*Note: With the long straights on this layout you can substitute eight 30-inch Straight Tracks (6-12042) and thirteen 10-inch Straight Tracks (6-12014).

SPACE REQUIRED: 14x19 feet

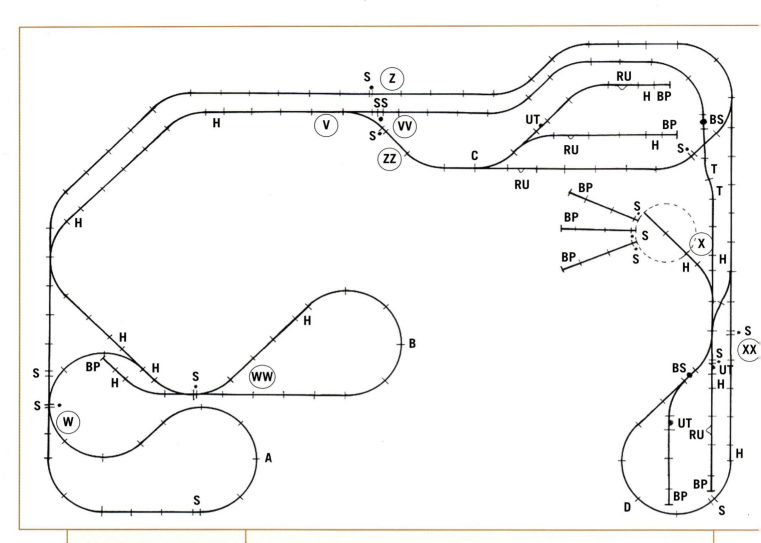

Add a fourth reverse loop and some yard tracks to complete a layout with four destination cities on four reverse loops. This one also has a turntable and a three-stall roundhouse. The letters V, VV, W, WW, X, XX, Z, and ZZ are where wires connect for eight electrically isolated blocks, as described in Chapter 3.

FASTRACK SECTIONS REQUIRED:

Quantity	Symbol	Part No.	Description
80*	None	6-12014	10-inch Straight Track
8	BP	6-12035	Lighted Bumper
or:			
8	BP	6-12059	Earthen Bumper
2	BS	6-12060	Block Section (insulated half-straight)
11	H	6-12024	Half-Straight
4	RU	6-12054	Operating Track
13	S	6102047350	1 3/8-inch Insulated Straight (furnished with 060 and 072 switches and as a replacement part; ballast shoulder on one side only)
2	T	6-12055	072 11 1/4-Degree Half-Curved Track
3	UT	6-12020	Uncoupling Track
14	36	6-12015	036 45-Degree Curved Track
1	36	6-12045	036 Remote Switch (Left Hand)
1	36	6-12046	036 Remote Switch (Right Hand)
1	45	6-12051	45-Degree Crossover

*Note: With the long straights on this layout you can substitute twenty-six 30-inch Straight Tracks (6-12042) and two 10-inch Straight Tracks (6-12014).

SPACE REQUIRED: 14x19 feet

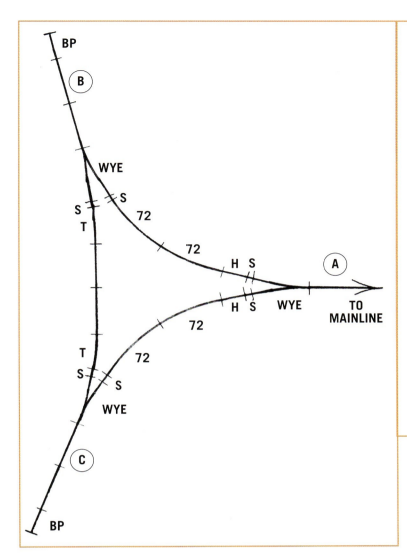

A wye for turning a single locomotive assembled with 072 wye switches and 072 curves.

FASTRACK SECTIONS REQUIRED:

Quantity	Symbol	Part No.	Description
6	None	6-12014	10-inch Straight Track
2	BP	6-12035	Lighted Bumper
or:			
2	BP	6-12059	Earthen Bumper
2	H	6-12024	Half-Straight
6	S	6102047	350 1 3/8-inch Insulated Straight (furnished with 072 switches and as a replacement part; ballast shoulder on one side only)
2	T	6-12055	072 11 1/4-Degree Half-Curved Track
3	Wye	6-12047	072 Wye Remote Switch
4	72	6-12041	072 22 1/2-Degree Curved Track

SPACE REQUIRED: 5x9 feet

Reversing Wyes

Real railroads use a special track arrangement called a wye to reverse complete trains at the ends of branch lines and in some terminals. Essentially, a wye is a triangular-shaped track arrangement. If the locomotive enters a wye from the left (A), it travels up one leg (B) to stop and back up, and then travels to the end of the second leg (C) and stops and backs up. When it resumes travel it exits the wye at the same place it entered but heads in the opposite direction. Unless you design a T-shaped model railroad, it is difficult to include a wye. There's a plan in this chapter for a basic wye using the FasTrack 072 Wye Remote Switch (6-12047). The stub ends are just long enough for a locomotive and, perhaps, a single car. The 14x19-foot main line track plan in Chapter 10 includes this same wye assembled from three 6-12047 switches.

There's also a wye assembled from 036 switches on the 14x19-foot plan in this chapter. That wye is really just a junction between the main line and the two reversing loops in the lower left of the plan.

Turntables for Reversing Locomotives

Some of the plans in Chapters 10 through 12, as well as the 14x19-foot plan in this chapter, include round turntables that can be used to turn locomotives. At this time Lionel does not make a turntable, but you can use a lazy Susan for a turntable, or you may find a model at your local dealer. You will have to devise some kind of circular electrical wiper and contact system to provide power for the turntable track while it rotates 360 degrees. There are some devices for HO and O scale model railroads that you may be able order through your Lionel dealer to accomplish the wiring for a turntable.

You can use a lazy Susan from a hardware or kitchen store to build a turntable. To convert an 18- or 24-inch-diameter lazy Susan into a turntable, just cut straight track to extend about one inch beyond the edges of the lazy Susan. You might be able to use standard (10-inch), half-length (5-inch), and 1 3/8-inch straights, but you may need to custom-cut a track section to be able to get the exact length. If you do, use that custom section in the middle of the lazy Susan.

Most lazy susans are a light pastel shade of beige or brown. You may want to paint it a dark brown or black so it looks more realistic. Attach the track with silicone caulking compound or Shoe Goo. The lazy Susan will probably be 1/4 inch or higher than the track. Simply elevate the tracks leading to and from the turntable with a stack of three or more pieces of 1/4x5/8-inch strips of balsa or basswood cut into 2 1/4-inch-long ties and died or painted black or dark brown. You will, of course, need to revolve the turntable by hand and hold it steady while the locomotive runs on and off the turntable track.

The simple method of wiring the turntable is to attach a track power wire to the center rail's tab on the bottom of the track and to the tab for one outside rail on the nearest powered track, and attach an alligator clip to the end of each wire. Connect the alligator clips to the turntable track's rails to match the connections at the Lockon. After the locomotive is run onto the turntable, turned, and run off, disconnect the alligator clips and attach them to the edges of the lazy Susan so they do not get tangled or touch each other and cause a short circuit.

An oval/double reverse loop and figure 8 all in one, with 036 curves and switches.

FASTRACK SECTIONS REQUIRED:

Quantity	Symbol	Part No.	Description
8	None	6-12014	10-inch Straight Track
4	H	6-12024	Half-Straight
4	N	6-12025	4 1/2-inch Straight Track
8	36	6-12015	036 45-Degree Curved Track
2	36	6-12045	036 Remote Switch (Left Hand)
2	36	6-12046	036 Remote Switch (Right Hand)
1	90	6-12019	90-Degree Crossover

SPACE REQUIRED: 3 1/2x7 1/2 feet

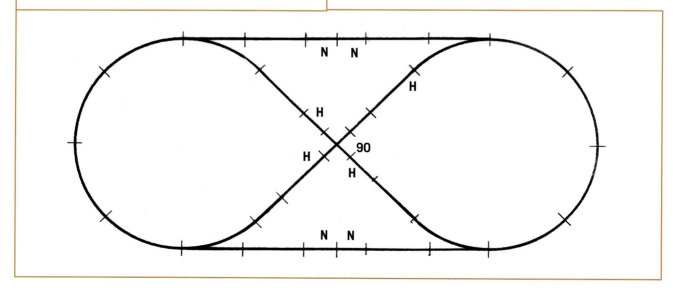

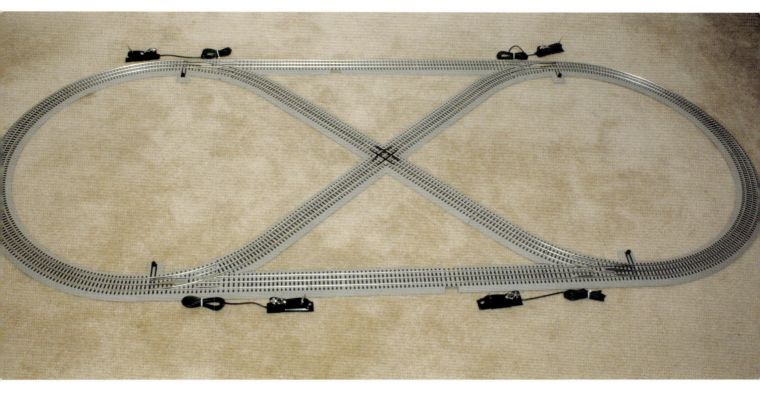

This compact layout combines the oval, figure-8, and overlapping reverse loop plans.

Overlapping Reverse-Loop Layouts

You can squeeze two reverse loops into a layout as small as 4x8 feet if you include them as part of a figure 8–plus oval layout like these. If you trace a train's path around these layouts you'll see that the train can take a diagonal route while traveling in either a clockwise or a counterclockwise direction to change its direction completely. Again, these plans are meant to be building blocks that you can expand by adding additional pairs of straights, by expanding and bending the plan into L-shapes, or by including the plan as part of a larger layout.

Two-Level Reverse-Loop Layouts

It is also possible to lay one reverse on top of the other like the 5x9-foot layout in Chapter 5. The tracks can be supported on the FasTrack Elevated Trestle Set (6-12038) or the FasTrack Graduated Trestle Set (6-12037).

Those overlapping loops can be on a single level, using a 45-degree and a 90-degree crossing, but that requires a minimum of 5 1/2x9 1/2 feet—just a smidge too large for a Ping-Pong table. The reverse loops can be assembled from any size curves, including 072 curves and switches.

7 1/2x15 1/2-Foot 072 Two-Level, Double-Loop Layout

This 072 plan with overlapping reverse loops needs about 7 1/2x15 1/2 feet of space. There is room for a widened girder bridge where the curves overlap to the right of the plan.

7x13-Foot 072 Two-Level, Double-Loop Layout

I only had 7x13 feet available, so I squeezed the 7 1/2x15 1/2-foot plan down. I also opted to replace one of the 072 switches with an 072 wye just for variety (it did not save any space). This compact plan requires that long stretches of curved track be placed directly above the curves on the lower level. There is no bridge that will support such long runs, but you can make your own. Buy enough extra pieces of track

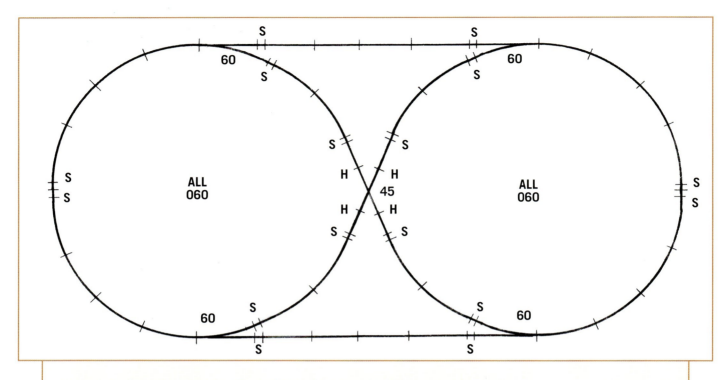

An oval, double reverse loop, and figure-8 plan all in one, with 060 curves and switches.

FASTRACK SECTIONS REQUIRED:

Quantity	Symbol	Part No.	Description
8	None	6-12014	10-inch Straight Track
4	H	6-12024	Half-Straight
16	S	6102047350	1 3/8-inch Insulated Straight (furnished with 060 switches and as a replacement part; ballast shoulder on one side only)
1	45	6-12051	45-Degree Crossover
24	60	6-12056	060 22 1/2-Degree Curved Track
2	60	6-12057	060 Remote Switch (Left Hand)
2	60	6-12058	060 Remote Switch (Right Hand)

SPACE REQUIRED: 5 1/2x11 1/2 feet

(072 curves, in this case) to span the gap. Cement these pieces upside down (ballast to ballast) beneath the bridge sections of track using Shoe Goo or clear silicone caulking. Stagger the joints a half-section apart (top versus bottom) so the upside-down track supports the track joints on the top track. Glue some of the tall bents from the 6-12038 Elevated Trestle set to the edges of the track so the bents are clear of the trains on the lower level. It's not elegant, but it works. An alternative is to simply cut some pieces of 5/8-inch plywood to the shape of the curves on the bridges.

The large 072 curves provide some spectacular scenes as the passenger and freight trains snake through the reverse loops, one train crossing effortlessly over the other.

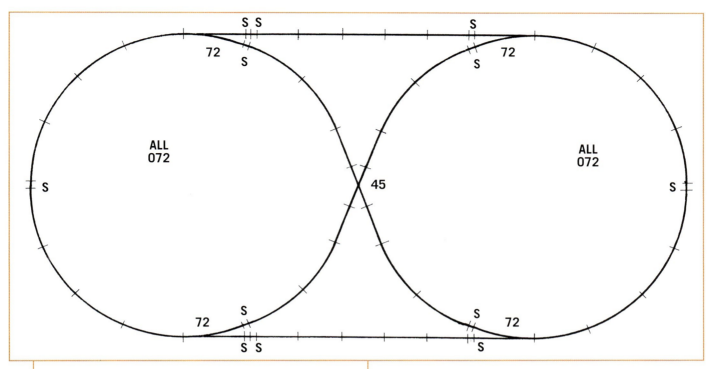

An oval, a double reverse loop, and figure-8 plan all in one, with 072 curves and switches.

FASTRACK SECTIONS REQUIRED:

Quantity	Symbol	Part No.	Description
14	None	6-12014	10-inch Straight Track
12	S	6102047350	1 3/8-inch Insulated Straight (furnished with 072 switches and as a replacement part; ballast shoulder on one side only)
1	45	6-12051	45-Degree Crossover
24	72	6-12041	072 22 1/2-Degree Curved Track
2	72	6-12048	072 Remote Switch (Left Hand)
2	72	6-12049	072 Remote Switch (Right Hand)

SPACE REQUIRED: 6 1/2x13 1/2 feet

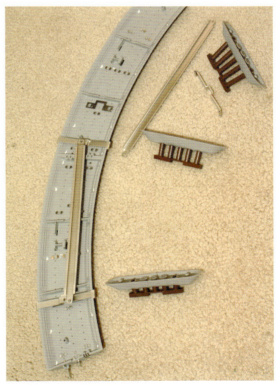

The Graduated Trestle Set (6-12037) includes 10-inch-long steel spacer bars to ensure that uphill slope is constant. Metal clips attach the individual trestle bent ends to the FasTrack ballast shoulders.

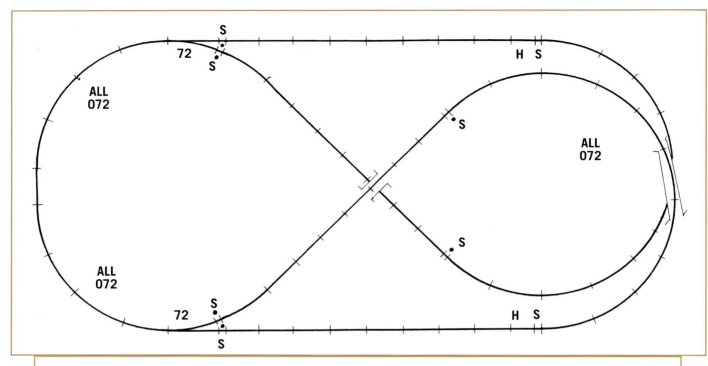

A two-level double reverse-loop-to-reverse-loop plan, with 072 curves and switches.

FASTRACK SECTIONS REQUIRED:

Quantity	Symbol	Part No.	Description
31*	None	6-12014	10-inch Straight Track
2	H	6-12024	Half-Straight
8	S	6102047350	1 3/8-inch Insulated Straight (furnished with 072 switches and as a replacement part; ballast shoulder on one side only)
30	72	6-12041	072 22 1/2-Degree Curved Track
1	72	6-12048	072 Remote Switch (Left Hand)
1	72	6-12049	072 Remote Switch (Right Hand)

*Note: With the long straights on this layout you can substitute eight 30-inch Straight Tracks (6-12042) and seven 10-inch Straight Tracks (6-12014).

SPACE REQUIRED: 7 1/2x15 1/2 feet

A condensed two-level double reverse-loop-to-reverse-loop plan, with 072 curves and switches.

FASTRACK SECTIONS REQUIRED:

Quantity	Symbol	Part No.	Description
9	None	6-12014	10-inch Straight Track
4	H	6-12024	Half-Straight
6	S	6102047350	1 3/8-inch Insulated Straight (furnished with 072 switches and as a replacement part; ballast shoulder on one side only)
3	T	6-12055	072 11 1/4-Degree Half-Curved Track
38	72	6-12041	072 22 1/2-Degree Curved Track
1	72	6-12048	072 Remote Switch (Left Hand)
1	Wye	6-12047	072 Wye Remote Switch

*Note: With the long straights on this layout you can substitute three 30-inch Straight Tracks (6-12042).

SPACE REQUIRED: 7x13 feet

I assembled this 7 1/2x13-foot two-level, two-loop layout with the upper loop temporarily resting on the rails of the lower loop.

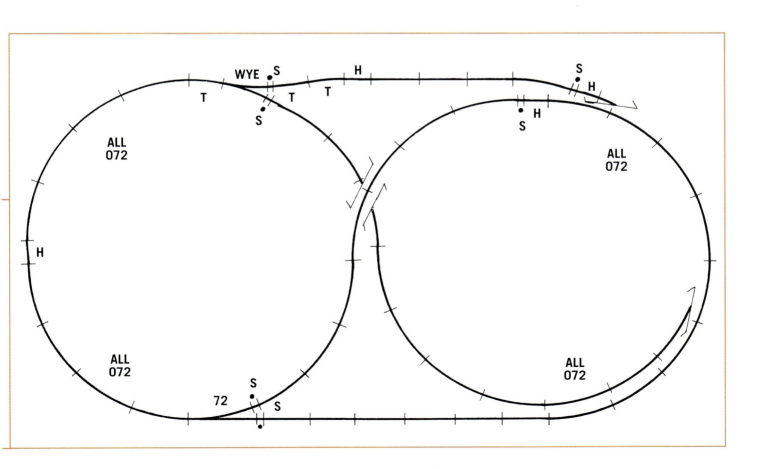

I used a full Elevated Trestle Set (6-12038) and a Truss Bridge with Flasher and Piers (6-12772) to support the upper-level track. Since the main line serves as both the up and down grade, I only need half of a Graduated Trestle Set (6-12037).

The bridges over the curves on the right and the ess-bend in the center were made by cementing pieces of 072 curve upside down to the bottom of the layout's 072 curved track sections. The joints are offset half a section so the upper and lower reinforce each other.

If you opt for TrainMaster Command Control locomotives and power supplies you can operate two, three, or even four trains at once on this layout with no block wiring.

The 072 curves are far more realistic than the tighter 036 and 048 curves, especially with longer passenger cars and large locomotives.

Do-It-Yourself Layout Design

Think of FasTrack as a jigsaw puzzle that you assemble into your dream railroad. You might view the plans in this book as you would view the photo on the puzzle's box—that is, the solution, an example of what the completed puzzle should look like. This FasTrack puzzle, however, is one that you can expand or modify to fill whatever size tabletop (or floor) you have.

The Geometry of FasTrack

The FasTrack system has a built-in design geometry to allow an infinite variety of layouts with each piece fitting perfectly. The smallest 36-inch curves require eight 45-degree sections per circle. The 60- and 72-inch curves are half of 45 degrees each, or 22 1/2 degrees, and the 84-inch curved sections are half the length of the 60- and 72-inch curves, or about 11 1/4 degrees. To match these, the 36-inch curves are available in half lengths (to match the spread of the 60- and 72-inch curves). The 36-inch curves are also available in 1/4-length pieces to match the 84-inch curves, and the 72-inch curves are also available in half lengths to match the 84-inch curves.

Four parallel loops of track run around the edges of Peter Perry's 10x24-foot layout. He designed the layout using the track sections themselves, rather than drawing it first.

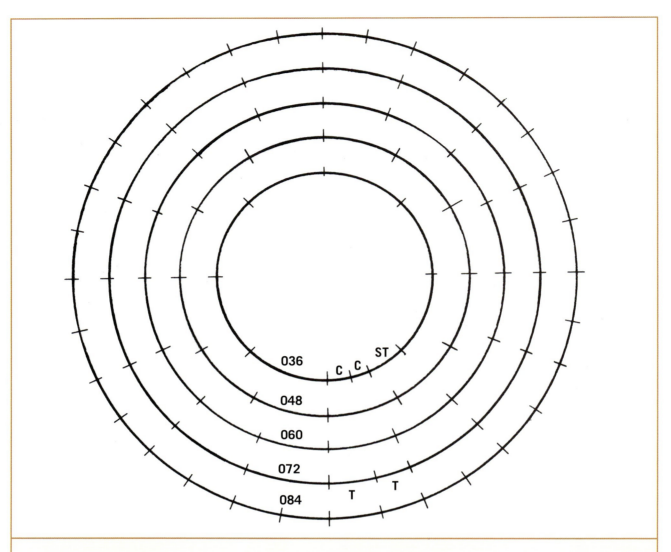

The 036, 060, 072, and 084 FasTrack curves are designed to be perfect segments of a circle, down to a segment as small as 11 1/4 degrees. Only the 048 curves have a different geometry (30 degrees of a circle), but they can interface with other sizes on 90- and 180-degree curves. The C tracks are 1/4-length 036 curves and the ST tracks are 1/2-length 036 curves. The T tracks are 1/2-length 072 curves.

The Perfect Fit

Lionel offers a range of short, straight FasTrack filler pieces that can be used to make up nearly any gap or misalignment. The key on pages 18 and 19 lists most of the FasTrack sections.

The first rule of laying track to your own design is to remember that any track section you add to one side of the layout must be matched with an identical length section on the opposite side of the layout. Hence, you will see a number of short S sections inserted in many of the plans. These are needed because there is usually

an S section (with a dot on the plans) on the opposite side of the circle. That dot means the short section is used as an insulating track as described in Chapter 3. You can, however, use this design to your advantage to increase the size of any plan in this book. Simply add as many pairs of straights as you wish (one straight on each side of any oval).

For compact layouts, matching switches are designed to replace one section of 36-inch curve track and one standard-length (10-inch) straight track. The 060 and 072 switches are also designed to

If you remove the two short curved pieces from two 036 switches (whether right-hand or left-hand), the switches can be joined to make a crossover with 6-inch on-center track spacing.

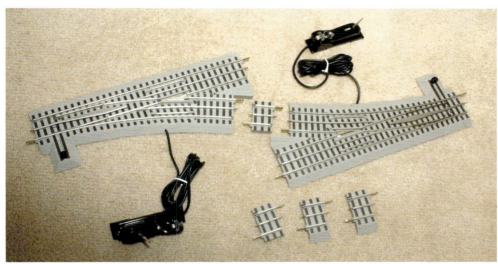

The 060 and 072 switches include three short (1 3/8 inch) straights. The short straight with no ballast shoulders is intended to be used between two switches (right-hand or left-hand) to assemble a crossover with parallel straight tracks spaced 6 inches apart on center.

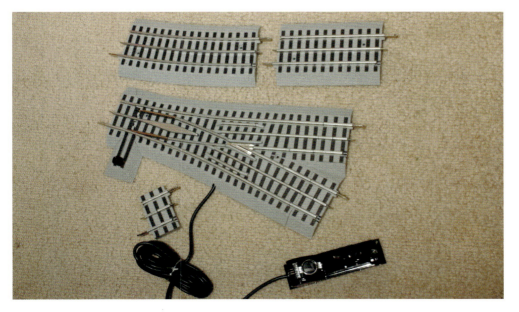

The FasTrack 072 Wye Remote Switch (6-12047) has curved routes that are the same length as a 072 11 1/4-Degree Half-Curved Track (6-12055 [top], T on the plans) plus a Half-Straight (6-12024 [top], H on the plans).

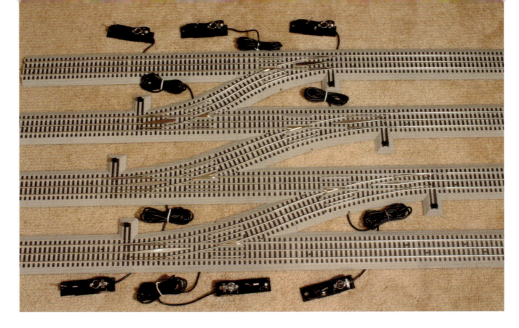

All FasTrack switches (top to bottom: 036, 060, and 072) have removable track sections so you can place two right-hand or two left-hand switches side-by-side and maintain a 6-inch on-center track spacing with any or all of the FasTack switches.

replace standard 060 or 072 curves as described in Chapter 6. You can, then, add a switch just about anywhere on the layout to create a siding or to lead to a diverging route. There is also a complete assortment of short filler track pieces, a plug-in terminal track, accessory-activating track, uncoupling track, operating track, grade crossings, end of track bumpers, and 45- and 90-degree crossings.

Expanding the Layout Plans

You can follow any of the plans in this book to the letter. The majority of them, however, are intended only as a basic step-off point. They usually occupy the smallest possible space to give you an idea of how much you can cram into the smallest area. Any of the plans can be enlarged and the smaller ones can be combined with other small plans to create much larger empires.

I suggest that you use the largest possible curves for your Lionel layout. The trains look far more realistic on 060 curves than they do on 036 or even 048 curves. Some of the largest Lionel locomotives will only operate on 072 or larger curves. Again, the layouts presented in these pages have the largest possible curves for the given space. Remember, too, that all of the curves, including switches and inner ovals, must be 072 or 084 for the largest locomotives to be able operate over the entire layout. If you do decide to use 036 and 048 curves, try to use 060 switches for the simple reason that they look far more realistic and require little more space.

An 8 1/2x16-Foot Triple-Track Main Line Layout

This triple-track main line layout is designed with 072 curves and larger so you can operate even the largest Lionel locomotive over it. The two outer curves are both 084 with short lengths of straight track to maintain that minimum 6-inch center-to-center track spacing. You can do just about anything with three trains on this layout, including reversing complete trains operating in either direction. The crossovers allow the trains to reach the reversing loops from any of the three main-line tracks, also without backing up. The electrical gaps are positioned as shown in Chapter 3 to allow the three trains to operate with conventional control.

Track Planning in Three Dimensions

You can use a compass, 45-degee and 30/60-degree drafting triangles, and an architect's ruler with different scales to draw your own plans. For most of us, however, it's far easier and quicker to use the track itself. You can purchase an assortment of straight track sections, quarter-circles of each of the different curves you feel might fit, and at least one sample of each of the different size switches you might want to include. Mark the outline of the track right on the tabletop. You will probably discover that you need some short straights or partial curves when you actually assemble the track, but your on-the-tabletop plan will help you determine how many pieces of each size and type of track you need.

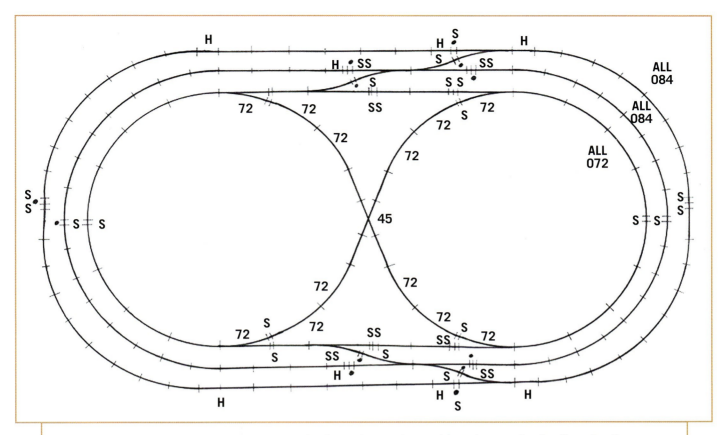

This triple-track main-line layout also has reversing loops that can be used for trains traveling in either direction.

FASTRACK SECTIONS REQUIRED:

Quantity	Symbol	Part No.	Description
32*	None	6-12014	10-inch Straight Track
24	None	6-12041	072 22 1/2-Degree Curved Track
8	H	6-12024	Half-Straight
38	S	6102047350	1 3/8-inch Insulated Straight (furnished with 072 switches and as a replacement part; ballast shoulder on one side only)
1	45	6-12051	45-Degree Crossover
6	72	6-12048	072 Remote Switch (Left Hand)
6	72	6-12049	072 Remote Switch (Right Hand)
64	84	6-12061	084 11 1/4-Degree Curved Track

*Note: With the long straights on this layout you can substitute six 30-inch Straight Tracks (6-12042) and fourteen 10-inch Straight Tracks (6-12014).

SPACE REQUIRED: 8 1/2x16 feet

Peter Perry's 10x24-foot FasTrack layout was designed on the tabletop. First he determined the size of the space he had available, then he assembled the track. He started with outermost loops of track using 072 curves. He then fit in three smaller concentric curves inside the outer oval, using 060, 048, and 036 curved track sections. There was room for a fifth egg-shaped oval inside the near end; the only switch on the entire layout leads to a stub-ended siding from that innermost oval. Each of the ovals has its own power supply.

FasTrack provides the practical means you can use to create your dream model railroad. Since the FasTrack system snaps together, you can expand your model railroad or even change the layout completely and as often as you wish.

CHAPTER 10

Tabletop Layouts for Room-Size Spaces

A ll of the layouts in this chapter are designed to be assembled on tabletops. There's no reason why you cannot assemble them on the floor, but the track placement is arranged to provide room for you to either walk around the layout or walk into it.

How Much Space Do I Need for a Layout?

The quick answer is "About three times as much space as you have." When you start dreaming about a Lionel layout, your dreams often create scenes that would require a basketball court to recreate. At the other end of that spectrum, you can assemble an exciting layout with room for two trains in as little as 4 1/2x7 feet. If you live in a small condo, 5x9 feet is enough to build a really creative layout, including the one in Chapter 5. That's the size of Ping-Pong tabletop and not much larger than a double bed. If you place one end of the 5x9 tabletop against the wall, it can fit above a double bed in even a very small bedroom and still leave room for furniture.

The reproduction double-track Hell Gate Bridge (6-32904) is on the upper level of Bill Langsdorf's 16x18-foot layout.

Lionel layouts are operated in a variety of different rooms ranging from a 10x11-foot bedroom to a basketball court–size warehouse. Some popular choices for a layout room include a basement den, all or part of a garage, an attic above a house or a garage, and a variety of separate buildings dedicated exclusively to Lionel FasTrack layouts.

Reaching that Derailed Train

When you build a permanent layout, consider how you are going reach the derailed trains. Most Lionel layouts are built on benchwork sturdy enough to walk on. Essentially, these are indoor patio decks but with a plywood tabletop deck. Most Lionel model railroaders also prefer a layout that is the usual tabletop height of about 30 inches from the floor so they can get an "aerial" view of the entire layout. If they want to get close, they simply sit on a chair or kneel beside the layout.

Portable FasTrack Layouts

In addition to using Ping-Pong and conference tables as described in Chapter 1, you can also assemble a lightweight portable tabletop with 1/8-inch plywood braced by 1x2s as shown in *The Lionel Train Book* and *The Big Book of Lionel Trains*. Two inches of extruded Styrofoam cemented firmly to the tabletop is extremely rugged and lightweight and will deaden the sound. I assembled a 4x6-foot tabletop so it would be small enough to get through a doorway. I then used two sawhorses with 30-inch legs to support the layout. If you want a larger layout with this system, I recommend building the tables no larger than 4 1/2x6 feet. Four of these tables will provide a 9x12-foot tabletop—large enough for any of the layouts in this book designed for 072 track.

Building a Tabletop for a FasTrack Layout

If you choose to build a permanent table for your Lionel FasTrack layout rather than using portable Ping-Pong tables, conference tables, or lightweight tabletops and sawhorses, be prepared to make the table strong and rugged. Bill Langdorf used 1x4s with 5/8-inch plywood (MDF is a good alternative to conventional plywood) tabletop for his 16x18-foot layout. Peter Perry used 2x4s with 3/8-inch plywood underlayment for the top. Both opted for 2x4 legs. The construction is similar to an outdoor patio deck with exterior framework and crossmembers placed about 2 feet apart. All the joints are secured with No. 8 woodscrews. The legs are secured in place with carriage bolts, nuts, and washers so they can be removed for transportation. I strongly suggest that you divide the total table area into segments no larger than 4 1/2x6 feet each so you can take the whole thing apart and move it through a standard doorway. Also, it's wise to paint all the wood framework and legs before installing the tabletop, then paint the tabletop on both sides and install it. Finally, cover the tabletop with your choice of sound-deadeners.

You can create two or more levels of track with uphill and downhill grades. Conventional HO scale model railroads feature tabletops cut out along the edges of the track. First, use a saber saw to cut through the plywood tabletop about 1/8 inch beyond the ends of the ties. The track that is to be elevated is then pulled upward, complete with the plywood below it, and the elevated section is supported on 1x4 risers screwed to the benchwork crossmembers. This system means that you can only use the track configuration you have created. For a FasTrack layout, I suggest leaving the tabletop flat (as in illustrations C and F) with no cutouts except, perhaps, for a small lake in what you know will always be the middle of any plywood panel.

Bill Langsdorf created an upper level by simply screwing some 2x6 pieces of lumber on edge to support a second deck. The diagram shows the sizes of the plywood sheets he cut for the lower level and the plywood sheets for the upper level. He uses the FasTrack 6-12037 Graduated Trestle Set to elevate the track from the lower to upper level as shown in Chapter 1. With this system he can rearrange the track on the lower and upper levels to any configuration, including the places where the lower and upper levels are linked by tracks on the Graduated Trestle bents.

Use No. 4 sheet-metal screws to secure the track to the tabletop, but tighten them only until the screw heads just touch the top of the ballast. If you overtighten the screws you can distort the track (or break

Traditional scenery methods include (C) and (F) supporting the track on 5/8-inch plywood with 1x4 risers and aluminum door screen covered with plaster and dyed sawdust for the scenery shapes (or, today, ground foam surface textures). The track can be hidden beneath the scenery (E) if you provide removable access panels. A few choices of bridges include a girder bridge (A), like the Die-Cast Metal Girder Bridge (6-14222); a wooden trestle (B), which could be added using groups of bents from Lionel's Elevated Trestle Set (6-12038) or Graduated Trestle Set (6-12037); and a steel truss bridge (D), like the Truss Bridge with Flasher and Piers (6-12772). *Courtesy Lionel LLC*

LAYOUT SUGGESTIONS

it), which can cause derailments. Langsdorf used 2-inch screws so they would reach through the soft 1-inch extruded Styrofoam layout top. Perry used 1 1/2-inch screws to reach through the Homasote tabletop to the plywood beneath.

The Realism of the Rumble and the Roar

One of the thrills of operating Lionel trains is the sound the locomotives and cars generate just rolling over the track. This is what power sounds like! FasTrack's hollow base can, however, create some levels of sound you might want to avoid. Most model railroaders who use FasTrack on a tabletop feel that there is a bit too much noise. There are at least four ways you can reduce the noise level and still retain that realistic rumble:

Cover the tabletop with sheets of 1/2-inch-thick Homasote wallboard. Homasote is almost identical to the gray cardboard on the back of old writing tablets and can be ordered by most lumberyards and building supply firms.

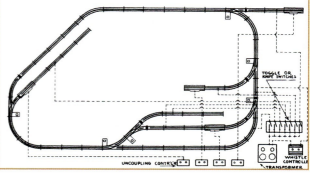

This 7x12-foot Coal Field Railroad layout was designed for Lionel's O-31 all-steel track. *Courtesy Lionel LLC*

Cover the tabletop with a layer of cork. In the Yellow Pages you can find dealers who sell rolls of sheet cork, or you may be able to find a bargain on cork floor tiles.

Cover the tabletop with a layer of 1-inch-thick extruded Styrofoam. The most common types are blue and pink. This is the least costly alternative and it works well, but the Styrofoam has little strength so

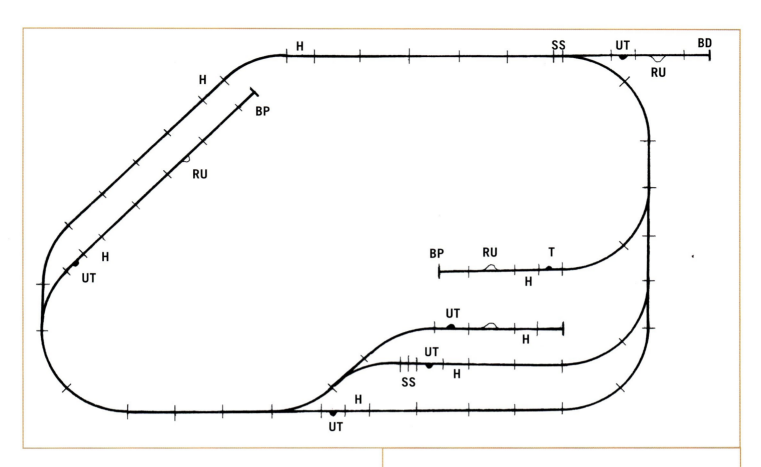

you will want a sturdy table beneath it. Generally, white Styrofoam is expanded rather than extruded and is much softer and far too easily damaged for use on a tabletop. Bill Langsdorf used 1-inch-thick extruded Styrofoam on his 14x18-foot layout in this chapter.

Cover the tabletop with rubberized antiskid mats that are used beneath area rugs. These mats are relatively inexpensive and work well. You can cover the mat with beige or green felt as we did on the 5x9-foot Ping-Pong layout in Chapter 5.

Scenery for Tabletop Layouts

The most important part of the scenery, the track and the ballast, is already incorporated into FasTrack. There are also FasTrack end-of track bumpers and bridges available. If you paint the tabletop a grass green, as Bill Langsdorf and Peter Perry have done, you only need a minimal amount of scenery to finish the layout. You can use traditional model railroad scenery-building techniques with aluminum door screen and patching plaster to extend your scale-size world outward from the ballast shoulders.

The FasTrack version of the "Coal Field Railroad" uses all 036 curves and switches.

FASTRACK SECTIONS REQUIRED:

Quantity	Symbol	Part No.	Description
7	H	6-12024	Half-Straight
23	None	6-12014	10-inch Straight Track
4	BP	6-12059	Earthen Bumper
or:			
4	BP	6-12035	Lighted Bumper
3	RU	6-12054	Operating Track
2	S	6102047350	1 3/8-inch Insulated Straight (furnished with 072 and 060 switches and as a replacement part; ballast shoulder on one side only)
1	SS	6-12026	1 3/4-inch Straight Track
6	UT	6-12020	Uncoupling Track
10	36	6-12015	036 45-Degree Curved Track
1	36	6-12045	036 Remote Switch (Left Hand)
5	36	6-12046	036 Remote Switch (Right Hand)

SPACE REQUIRED: 7x12 feet

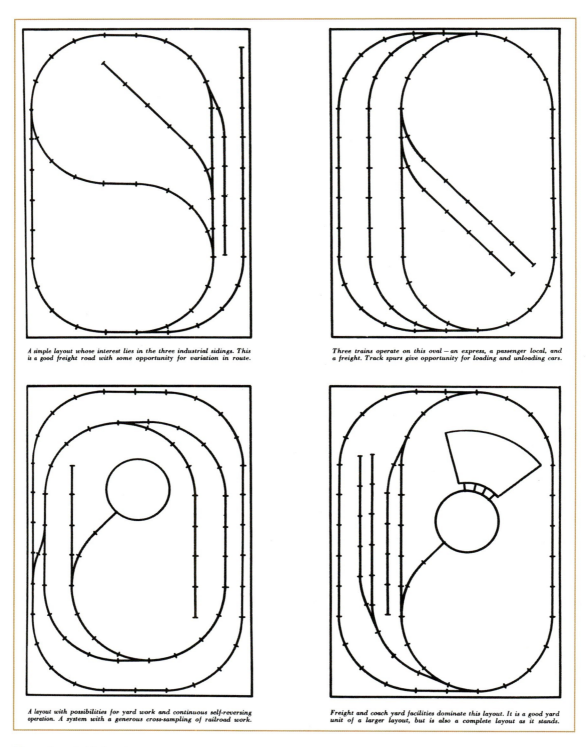

A simple layout whose interest lies in the three industrial sidings. This is a good freight road with some opportunity for variation in route.

Three trains operate on this oval — an express, a passenger local, and a freight. Track spurs give opportunity for loading and unloading cars.

A layout with possibilities for yard work and continuous self-reversing operation. A system with a generous cross-sampling of railroad work.

Freight and coach yard facilities dominate this layout. It is a good yard unit of a larger layout, but is also a complete layout as it stands.

These four 9x12-foot layouts were designed for O-72-inch all-steel track, but you can use FasTrack 072 curves and switches if you remove the two short pieces of track from every switch. The tracks that connect the diverging ends of the switches need to be cut at the corners to clear the switches' ballast shoulders.
Courtesy Lionel LLC

For a FasTrack layout, I suggest that you consider making the scenery as movable as the track. If you create plaster scenery you are stuck with just one track arrangement unless you are willing to tear into the plaster and roadbed—a messy process. Luckily, there are alternatives to the screen-and-plaster approach, including Woodland Scenics–brand white Styrofoam and plaster-soaked gauze known as Scenic Cloth.

The materials used for scenery on the 5x9-foot portable layout in Chapter 5 works even better on a larger layout, whether portable or permanent. I suggest using green or beige felt (shaded with green paint) for the areas between the tracks. You can tuck crumpled newspapers under the felt for hills. When the scenery shapes are what you wish them to be, use scissors to trim the felt about 1/2 inch over the centerlines of all the track. Loosen the track-retaining screws and tuck the felt beneath the edges of the roadbed then retighten the screws. You can cut lake- or harbor-shaped holes (you decide on the shape) into the plywood or, if you opted for Homasote or Styrofoam on the top of the plywood, you can simply cut into the material for the lake or harbor. Cut a sheet of 1/8-inch Masonite to the shape of lake or harbor shore, paint it a dark greenish blue (Polly Scale's model railroad "Engine Black" is about the right shade), and apply several coats of clear gloss enamel or two-part epoxy decoupage fluids. Bring

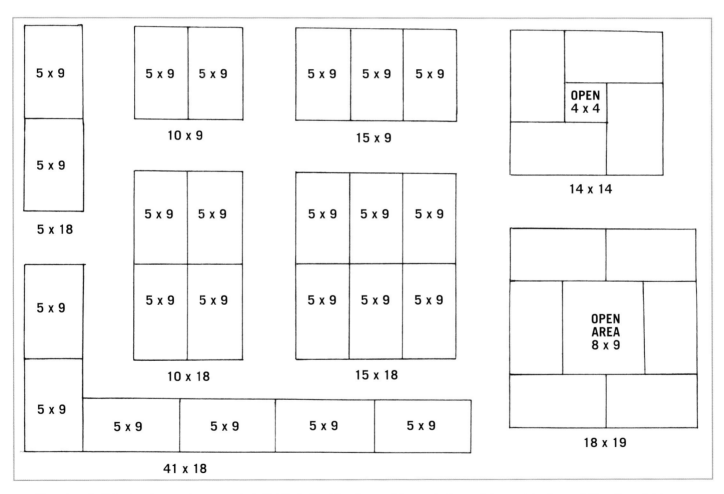

The plans in this chapter can be expanded slightly to fit at least one of these eight possible combinations of Ping-Pong tables for a sturdy-but-portable layout. The configurations can also be used for plywood tabletops since plywood is available in 4 1/2x5-foot sheets (half the size of a Ping-Pong table). The configurations can also be replicated with pairs of 2 1/2x8-foot folding conference tables.

the felt to the water's edge and add some real rocks and model railroad lichen to cover the seam.

The 7x12-Foot Coal Field Railroad

This "Coal Field Railroad" layout is one of a series that appeared in the late-1930s in Lionel's *Model Builder* magazine. Many were republished in the *Handbook for Model Builders* in 1940; three of these layouts are reproduced here, together with new versions of the plans to recreate the layouts with FasTrack. This 7x12-foot layout features a coal mine in the upper right and a classic Lionel 97 Electric Coaling Station at the mid-right to accept coal from the mine and transfer the load into other hoppers. There's also a power plant at the lower left and a coal dealer trestle at the upper right, as well as a passenger station along the forward edge and a series of passenger platforms along the upper edge of the layout. The wiring diagram shows seven on-off switches (SPSTs) to control power to two main line blocks and five sidings. With this wiring you can park a locomotive on any of the seven track areas or blocks (see Chapter 3) while operating a second train.

I revised the Coal Field Railroad to accept 036 FasTrack and switches. There is little change compared to the original plan, and I did not include any block wiring. You can utilize the same number of blocks that Lionel did or simply isolate the lower passing siding as described in Chapter 3.

The *Handbook for Model Builders* included dozens of track plans. The series of four included here was intended for use with traditional O-72 all-steel track. You can use the plan as-is for FasTrack 072 curves and switches, but the short straights furnished with the FasTrack switches have to be removed and every piece of track that adjoins the diverging ends of the switch must be cut so the ballast shoulder clears the 072 switch. Lionel does not offer a turntable, but you can construct one as described in Chapter 8.

Playing with Ping-Pong Tables

You can probably envision the size of a Ping-Pong table—about 2 feet longer and 1 foot wider than a double bed. The illustration included here shows eight different combinations of 5x9-foot tables. Most of the track plans in this chapter will fit on one or more of these configurations. The track plans are designed for the minimum possible space to accept that plan but can be expanded infinitely by adding pairs of straight tracks on opposite sides of the layout.

The "Well-Type Attic System" for FasTrack 036 curves and 036 switches.

FASTRACK SECTIONS REQUIRED:

Quantity	Symbol	Part No.	Description
7	H	6-12024	Half-Straight
75*	None	6-12014	10-inch Straight Track
7	BP	6-12059	Earthen Bumper
or:			
7	BP	6-12035	Lighted Bumper
1	RU	6-12054	Operating Track
6	S	6102047350	1 3/8-inch Insulated Straight (furnished with 072 and 060 switches and as a replacement part; ballast shoulder on one side only)
1	SS	6-12026	1 3/4-inch Straight Track
3	UT	6-12020	Uncoupling Track
27	36	6-12015	036 45-Degree Curved Track
7	36	6-12045	036 Remote Switch (Left Hand)
4	36	6-12046	036 Remote Switch (Right Hand)

*Note: With the long straights on this layout you can substitute sixteen 30-inch Straight Tracks (6-12042) and twenty-seven 10-inch Straight Tracks (6-12014).

SPACE REQUIRED: 13x13 feet

Pick a plan that is slightly smaller than the space you have available and expand it by adding another loop of track around the outside of the plan or additional passing sidings to one or more of the outer edges of the plan.

If you have the space, you can use two or more Ping-Pong tables arranged in a larger rectangle, a long row, or in an L, U, or O shape. Even if you opt for a permanent layout, you might consider assembling separate 4 1/2x5-foot tables so you can simply unbolt them from one another if you wanted to move the layout.

Two Ping-Pong tables placed side by side give you a 10x9-foot area, while two placed end to end produce a 5x18-foot area. Three Ping-Pong tables placed side by side produce a 9x15-foot area—large enough for slightly expanded versions of the 9x12-foot plans in this chapter for 072 track. You can use four Ping-Pong tables to create a solid 10x18-foot rectangle or six to create a 15x18-foot rectangle.

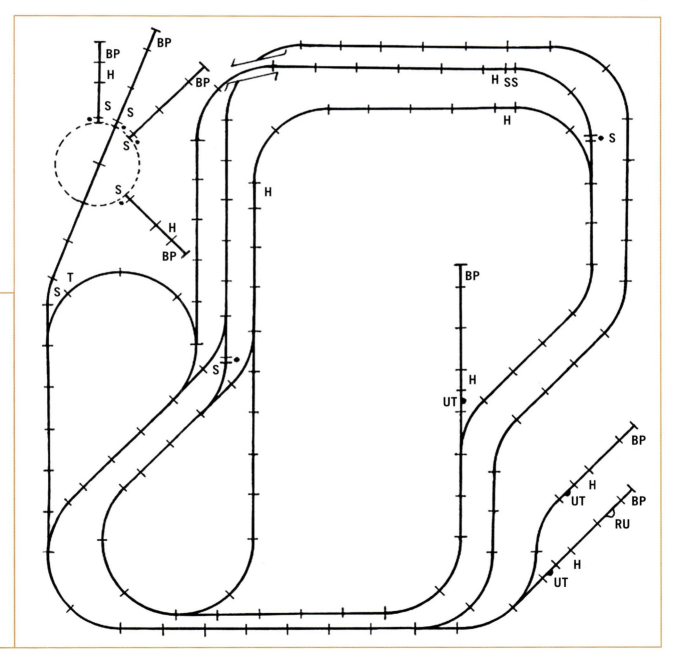

Abut the 5-foot ends against the 9-foot sides and you can also arrange four Ping-Pong tables into a 14-foot rectangle with a 4-foot-square access opening in the center. Or, six of them arranged in an oval will be 18x19 feet with a 5x9 access area in the middle. If you arrange two Ping-Pong tables in an L-shape, the layout will require 5x14 feet. You can extend either leg of that L to any length; the layout in the illustration uses 5x9-foot tabletops in an 18x41-foot corner (which might just fit in part of a basement den).

Room-Size Track Plans for the 13x13-Foot Well-Type Attic System

This is another layout from the *Handbook for Model Builders*. The "Well-Type Attic System" layout was published in two versions: this one to create a 13x13-foot layout, and a larger 13x18-foot version. The original plan for the 13x18 version was republished

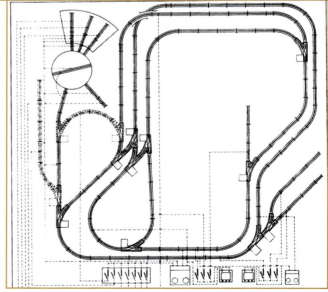

This 13x13-foot "Well-Type Attic System" was designed in the late 1930s for Lionel's O-31 all-steel track. *Courtesy Lionel LLC*

on page 54 of both *The Lionel Train Book* and *The Big Book of Lionel*. The larger version has an operating and access opening in the center. There is room on this 13x13 version for a 3x8-foot center access opening, but it is not shown on the drawing. There's an interesting over-and-under section along the rear portion of the layout. This layout also features Lionel's 97 Electric Coaling Station in the lower left but has no provision for a siding to dump coal into the hopper. I suggest locating the Electric Coaling Station in place of the station and simply moving the station to the inside of the track. The dashed lines indicate wires to the electrically isolated track blocks. The layout is divided into 12 blocks; four on the main line, four for the roundhouse and turntable, and four for industrial sidings. Note that the wire to the turntable track is a jumper from the inbound track.

Continued on page 134

The 14x18-foot "Lumber City Limited" is dedicated to recreating movements of logs and lumber. There's a separate oval logging railroad in the upper right. *Courtesy Lionel LLC*

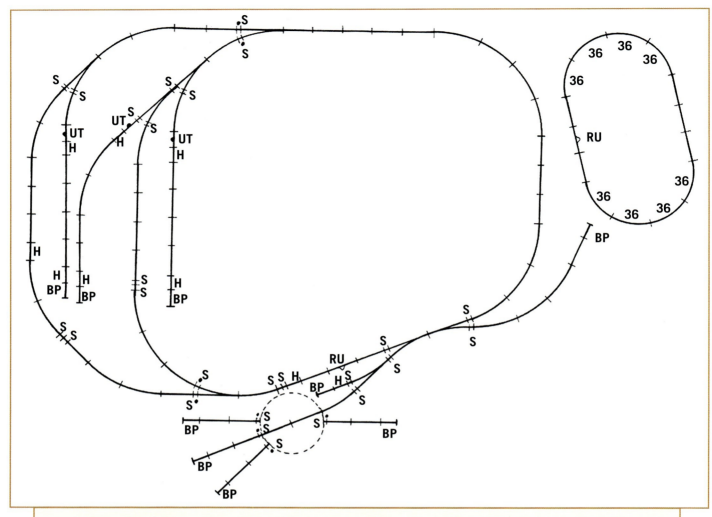

This version of the "Lumber City Limited" is designed for FasTrack 072 curves and 072 switches, except for the 036 curves on the logging railroad.

FASTRACK SECTIONS REQUIRED:

Quantity	Symbol	Part No.	Description
47*	None	6-12014	10-inch Straight Track
9	BP	6-12059	Earthen Bumper
or			
9	BP	6-12035	Lighted Bumper
8	H	6-12024	Half-Straight
2	RU	6-12054	Operating Track
26	S	6102047350	1 3/8-inch Insulated Straight (furnished with 072 switches and as a replacement part; ballast shoulder on one side only)
3	UT	6-12020	Uncoupling Track
8	36	6-12015	036 45-Degree Curved Track
27	None	6-12041	072 22 1/2-Degree Curved Track
4	None	6-12048	072 Remote Switch (Left Hand)
3	None	6-12049	072 Remote Switch (Right Hand)

*Note: With the long straights on this layout you can substitute six 30-inch Straight Tracks (6-12042) and twenty-eight 10-inch Straight Tracks (6-12014).

SPACE REQUIRED: 14x18 feet

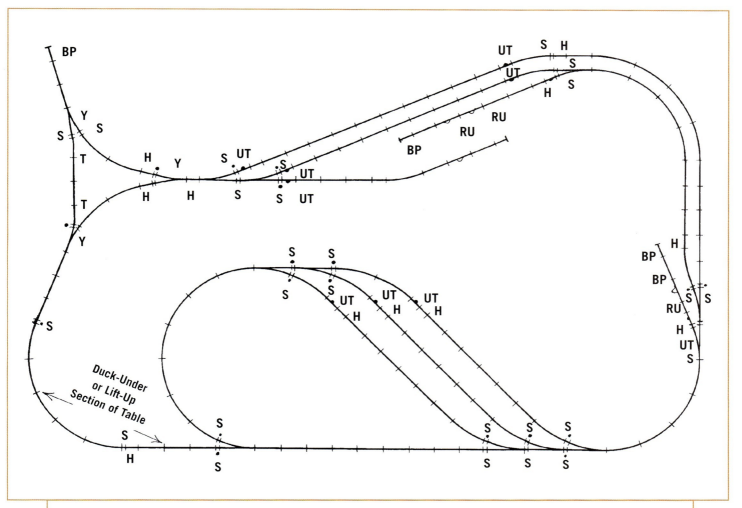

This "Point-To-Point" layout incorporates the three-track through yard and wye (upper left) from plans in other chapters. It is designed to be built for walk-in access through the lower left. All curves and switches are FasTrack 072.

FASTRACK SECTIONS REQUIRED:

Quantity	Symbol	Part No.	Description
74*	None	6-12014	10-inch Straight Track
4	BP	6-12059	Earthen Bumper
or:			
4	BP	6-12035	Lighted Bumper
12	H	6-12024	Half-Straight
4	RU	6-12054	Operating Track
31	S	6102047350	1 3/8-inch Insulated Straight (furnished with 072 switches and as a replacement part; ballast shoulder on one side only)
10	UT	6-12020	Uncoupling Track
38	None	6-12041	072 22 1/2-Degree Curved Track
5	None	6-12048	072 Remote Switch (Left Hand)
6	None	6-12049	072 Remote Switch (Right Hand)
3	Y	6-12047	072 Wye Remote Switch

*Note: With the long straights on this layout you can substitute sixteen 30-inch Straight Tracks (6-12042) and twenty-six 10-inch Straight Tracks (6-12014).

SPACE REQUIRED: 14x19 feet

Peter Perry has all the scenery he will ever want with his simple green-painted Homasote tabletop surface. These three tunnels are post–World War II Lionel with accessories from the same era, including a No. 40 flagpole from 1927, a No. 93 Silver Water Tower from 1931, and a No. 184 Bungalow from 1923.

The benchwork for Peter Perry's layout is solid 2x4 lumber throughout. *Peter Perry*

The tabletop on Peter Perry's 10x24-foot FasTrack layout is 3/8-inch underlayment plywood with a 1/2-inch Homasote surface. *Peter Perry*

Peter Perry's layout was assembled to fit right on the tabletop. There is no track plan. It is, essentially, five completely independent loops of track with no crossovers. The outer loops are 036, 048, 060, and 072 curves. The small oval is mostly 036 and 048 curves.

Most of the accessories on Peter Perry's layout are pre–World War II, but the trains are from all of Lionel's postwar era, including some of the latest locomotives and rolling stock.

Continued from page 129

You can devise a wiper system to pick up power from two 360-degree metal discs to power the turntable.

The FasTrack version of the well-type layout is nearly identical to the original. On this layout, one power pack can be dedicated the innermost oval and reverse loop and the second pack to the rest of the track as shown in Chapter 3. You can decide how many blocks you want for the layout or use no blocks at all and operate with TrainMaster Command Control.

The 14x18-Foot Lumber City Limited Layout

The 14x18-foot Lumber City Limited is a third layout from the *Handbook for Model Builders*. This one is my personal dream empire, partially because of the elevated oval of track in the upper right that represents a logging short line. Logs are dumped into the pond and floated across the lake to the sawmill. You can simply provide enough tilt to the hard surface of the pond so the logs roll across the surface to the sawmill. Leave a slot under the edge of the sawmill large enough so the logs roll off the table into a waiting box to be reloaded (by hand) into the logging railroad's log-dump cars.

Once again there's Lionel's 97 Electric Coaling Station in the lower center. The passenger station has two rows of station platforms, and there's a lumber dealer across from the station to accept loads of lumber on flatcars or in boxcars from the sawmill. No open center access is shown, but there's room for a 6x7-foot open area in the center of the layout.

The layout is divided into 12 electrically isolated blocks to operate two or more trains plus a completely independent system for the oval logging railroad. The main line is a single block with a second block for the passing siding like the simple oval in Chapter 3. Three of the blocks are for the roundhouse and turntable area (in this case, the four tracks around the turntable each feed power to the entry/exit track).

Room-Size Track Plan for a 14x19-Foot Shelf-Style Layout

This 14x19-foot plan is designed to be built on three shelves (right, top, and left) and a peninsula. It incorporates a reversing loop with three yard tracks, a long siding to simulate part of a double-track main line, and a wye in the upper left to reverse trains. Model railroaders would operate this as a point-to-point railroad with trains starting at the reverse loop's yard and running counterclockwise to the wye, where the locomotive alone would be reversed. The train would be a rearranged with a caboose at the opposite end and the locomotive would couple to the new head end of the train to pull it back to the three-track reverse loop yard. The track in the lower left allows oval-style operation around the extreme edges of the layout. You might have the train run two or three complete laps of the layout (changing the names of the towns two or three times as it passes and repasses through them). The track in the lower left can be built on a narrow section of benchwork or provided with a hinge and latch so it can be lifted for walk-in access to the center operating area. Frankly, this plan is just a suggestion so you can see how you can combine similar elements to custom-design a layout to fit your own space.

Peter Perry's 10x24-Foot FasTrack Layout

Peter Perry has been collecting Lionel equipment for most of his life, amassing an assortment of Lionel's most colorful stamped-metal tinplate stations, operating accessories, lights, and power poles. This pre–World War II array of miniatures is the appropriate setting for his much later Lionel locomotives and rolling stock.

After building several smaller layouts, he decided to create a piece of furniture (albeit massive) to fill half of his basement den. He hired a professional carpenter to assemble his benchwork to his specifications. The layout is a 10x24-foot trapezoidal shape to leave space for the fireplace and chairs behind the layout. The supports for the tabletop are framed like a patio deck from 2x4 lumber screwed and bracketed together. The legs are 2x4s to elevate the tabletop to 30 inches. The tabletop is 3/8-inch underlayment plywood covered with 1/2-inch Homasote wallboard. The entire layout is painted a grass green with a wood trim and fascia. All of the wiring is routed through holes in the table to terminal strips beneath the layout.

Perry likes to watch trains run and the more he can run at once, the happier it makes him. He snapped FasTrack together to fill the 10x24-foot space with a kidney-shaped outer oval using 072 track. He then created parallel tracks inside with 060, 048, and 036 curves for a four-track main line reminiscent of the Pennsylvania Railroad's trackage through the Northeast Corridor, Perry's childhood home. There's a much smaller fifth oval assembled from 036 and 048 curves inside one end of the layout. There are no switches in the four outer ovals—each of the five ovals is completely independent from the others. A single switch leads from the inner oval to a long siding that serves the operating accessories. Perry uses two postwar 275-watt ZW transformers to operate the four outer loops and a prewar 250-watt Z transformer to operate the accessories, with a small 80-watt CW80 for the small oval.

Bill Langsdorf's 16x18-Foot FasTrack Layout

Bill Langsdorf collects post–World War II and later Lionel equipment. He discovered TrainMaster Command Control and now operates a number of TMCC-equipped locomotives. His layout is completely wired to accept TrainMaster Command Control, including the ability to operate the switches and action accessories from the hand-held TrainMaster CAB-1 control. The track is, essentially, five loops, each with its own power supply. With TrainMaster Command Control, the trains can run anywhere that has power because the signals are received at the locomotives. His electrical components are illustrated in Chapter 3.

The support for the 16x18-foot layout is framed from 1x4 lumber with 2x4 legs. The tabletop is 5/8-inch plywood with a layer of 1-inch pink extruded Styrofoam insulation board on top. The 2x4 legs are tall enough to support the upper level track 39 inches from the floor. Langsdorf modified a track plan from Stan Trzoniec's book, *Toy Train Layout from Start to Finish*, to fill his available space. A single track leads from the lower upper level and a second track leads back down. These uphill and downhill tracks are supported by the FasTrack Graduated Trestle Set (6-12037).

The operating side of Bill Langsdorf's 16x18-foot FasTrack layout. The lower level is on the tabletop with a second upper level occupying about two-thirds of the area.

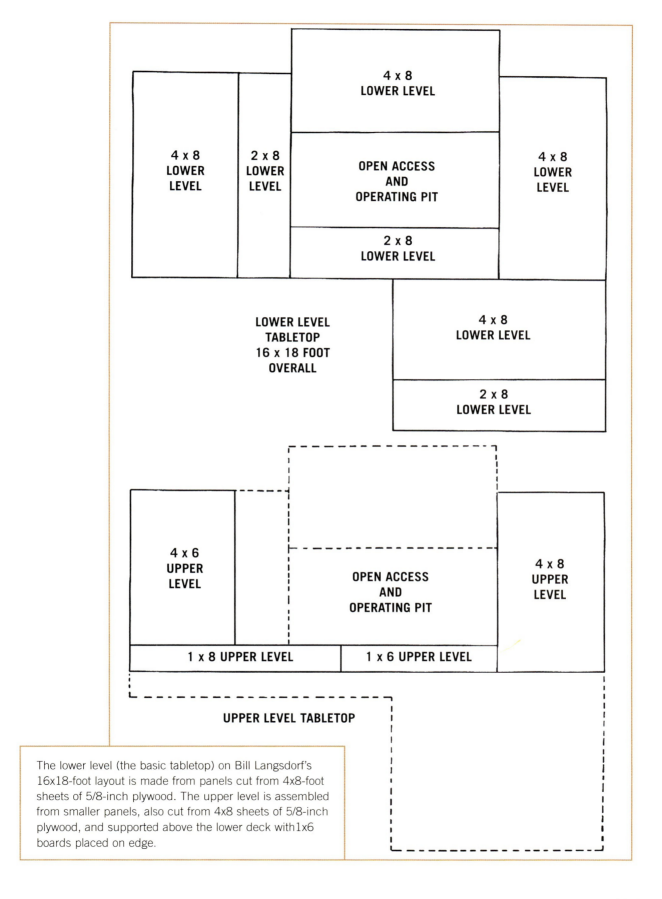

4 x 8
LOWER LEVEL

4 x 8
LOWER
LEVEL

2 x 8
LOWER
LEVEL

OPEN ACCESS
AND
OPERATING PIT

4 x 8
LOWER
LEVEL

2 x 8
LOWER LEVEL

LOWER LEVEL
TABLETOP
16 x 18 FOOT
OVERALL

4 x 8
LOWER LEVEL

2 x 8
LOWER LEVEL

4 x 6
UPPER
LEVEL

OPEN ACCESS
AND
OPERATING PIT

4 x 8
UPPER
LEVEL

1 x 8 UPPER LEVEL

1 x 6 UPPER LEVEL

UPPER LEVEL TABLETOP

The lower level (the basic tabletop) on Bill Langsdorf's 16x18-foot layout is made from panels cut from 4x8-foot sheets of 5/8-inch plywood. The upper level is assembled from smaller panels, also cut from 4x8 sheets of 5/8-inch plywood, and supported above the lower deck with 1x6 boards placed on edge.

Bill Langsdorf left this 2-foot-wide access aisle along most of the rear wall, as well as a 4x8-foot center access and operating pit.

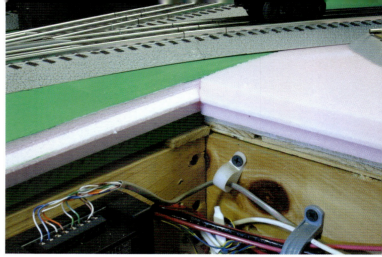

The tabletops on both the lower and upper levels of Bill Langsdorf's layout are 5/8-inch plywood covered with a 1-inch layer of pink extruded Styrofoam insulation board.

The upper deck of Bill Langsdorf's layout is supported by 1x6 boards placed on edge.

Right: The 1x6 supports for the upper deck on Bill Langsdorf's layout are hidden behind removable Plastruct-brand plastic sheets of simulated stone facades.

CHAPTER 11

Layouts for the Floor

Lionel FasTrack is rugged enough be assembled on the floor. With a floor-level layout you have access to any part of the layout by merely stepping between the tracks. That freedom means you can extend the tracks all the way to the walls of the room. The layout can be permanent if you have no other use for the space, or it can be portable and all or part of it can be packed away when there are other uses for the area.

If you do assemble a layout on the floor, try to find an area that is either completely bare or wall-to-wall carpet. If you must run track from a bare floor up onto a rug, fold some scraps of thin cardboard to about the size and shape of a matchbook and insert them between the track and the floor to support the track as it rises from the bare floor to the level of the carpet.

The 6 1/2x8-Foot Coal Field Railroad, One Step at a Time

A FasTrack layout usually begins with enough pieces to assemble an oval. I used 060 curves and switches for this layout because the trains look more realistic on the larger curves than on the 036 or even 048 curves that are more typical of simple oval layouts.

Beige felt, with patches of green, is used as the portable "earth" for this layout.

You can set up a model railroad on the floor with scenes this realistic.

The simple outer oval for the "Coal Field Railroad" uses 15 pieces of 060 curved track and six standard 10-inch Straight Track (6-12014) sections.

I expanded this layout with a cardboard street, a few Life-Like and Faller trees, a Lionel Bungalow (6-34121), a Lionel Suburban House (6-34108), a Lionel Large Suburban House (6-34113), and a Lionel Automatic Gateman (6-14091).

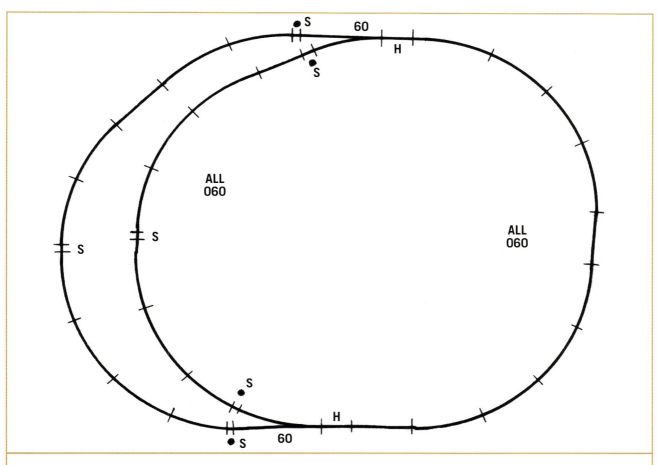

This FasTrack version of the "Coal Field Railroad" in Chapter 10 uses 060 curves.

FASTRACK SECTIONS REQUIRED:

Quantity	Symbol	Part No.	Description
4	None	6-12014	10-inch Straight Track
2	H	6-12024	Half-Straight
6	S	6102047350	1 3/8-inch Insulated Straight (furnished with 060 switches and as a replacement part; ballast shoulder on one side only)
22	60	6-12056	060 22 1/2-Degree Curved Track
1	60	6-12057	060 Remote Switch (Left Hand)
1	60	6-12058	060 Remote Switch (Right Hand)

SPACE REQUIRED: 6 1/2x8 feet

The same portable scenery techniques used for the 5x9-foot layout on a Ping-Pong table in Chapter 5 were used here. The felt is, of course, optional; but it does provide more realism than bare carpet. If you set up on bare wood or tile floor, I suggest that you cover the area with a 6 1/2x8-foot piece of the antiskid material used beneath area rugs. The antiskid mat and the felt will deaden the sound from the track so the trains retain that realistic "rumble and roar."

The 6 1/2x8-Foot Coal Field Railroad

This is the FasTrack version of the Coal Field Railroad from the 1940 *Handbook for Model Builders* that is also in Chapter 10. This version, however, was

Add a couple of switches and a few more pieces of track to create a passing siding. You can add a few action accessories like this #755 Talking Station (6-49812) and a #38 Water Tower.

assembled with 60-inch curves and switches to better accommodate larger locomotives and longer cars. The original plan was designed for all O-31 switches and curves, and the FasTrack version in Chapter 10 is designed for 036 curves and switches.

The 7 1/2x17 1/2-Foot Five-Train Christmas Dream Layout

The double figure 8 on page 147 is essentially the kind of layout I like to set up at Christmas time. This one is a variation on the plans in Chapter 6. It is assembled with 072 curves to accomodate any Lionel locomotive.

The layout on page 150 is designed so a tree goes inside the 036 figure 8 and the rest of the layout extends out into the den. There are no switches connecting the five tracks, so five transformers are used to operate five trains at a time. The two 45-degree crossings and the ess curve in the 084 outer oval lend interest to what is a very basic layout.

Basement-Size Layouts

If you have a 20x40-foot basement you might not want to fill it with a table. Many Lionel modelers assemble permanent layouts right on the floor. I strongly suggest, however, that you carpet the area, both for appearance and to deaden the sound. If you

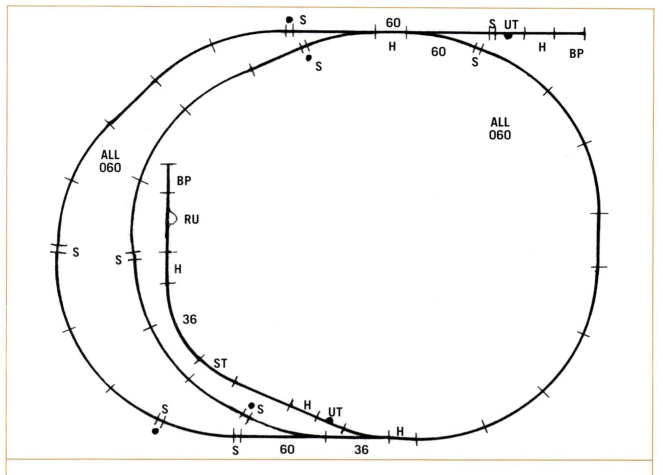

This FasTrack version of the "Coal Field Railroad" in Chapter 10 uses 060 curves and switches for the mainline, with 036 curves and switch on the industrial siding.

FASTRACK SECTIONS REQUIRED:

Quantity	Symbol	Part No.	Description
2	None	6-12014	10-inch Straight Track
2	BP	6-12059	Earthen Bumper
or			
2	BP	6-12035	Lighted Bumper
4	H	6-12024	Half-Straight
1	RU	6-12054	Operating Track
9	S	6102047350	1 3/8-inch Insulated Straight (furnished with 060 switches and as a replacement part; ballast shoulder on one side only)
1	ST	6-12022	Half-Curved Track (036 22 1/2-Degree)
2	UT	6-12020	Uncoupling Track
1	36	6-12015	036 45-Degree Curved Track
1	36	6-12046	036 Remote Switch (Right Hand)
21	60	6-12056	060 22 1/2-Degree Curved Track
1	60	6-12057	060 Remote Switch (Left Hand)
2	60	6-12058	060 Remote Switch (Right Hand)

SPACE REQUIRED: 6 1/2x8 feet

I added a low hill made from some Mountains in Minutes Flexrock and a pile of Life-Like trees. The long industrial siding uses a 036 switch and 036 curves to give the siding the appearance of a less-used track than the mainline.

The Union Pacific 2-8-0 and the F3A and F3B diesels are equipped with TrainMaster Command Control to operate the two trains on the layout. There's room for more accessories, including a 3472 Automatic Refrigerated Milk Car with Platform (upper left), 97 Electric Coaling Station (6-32921), and three Station Platforms (6-24190), so the layout looks very much like the dream layout from the Coal Field Railroad in the *Handbook for Model Builders* as shown in Chapter 10.

have that much space, use 072 and 084 curves and 072 turnouts like these plans. Either of the two layouts on page 151 is excellent for a floor-level model railroad. The 14 1/2x30-foot layout has ample room between the tracks for you or your guests to step in and out. It also has reverse loops for trains traveling in either direction. The tracks are connected by turnouts, so it's difficult to operate two trains unless you opt for TrainMaster Command Control.

The 10 1/2x38-foot layout on the left has a three-track through yard and a four-track stub-ended yard and diagonal reverse loop cut-off tracks to reverse trains from either direction. There are two large rectangular-shaped ovals so blocks can be installed to allow two trains to run on the ovals while a third switches the two yards. With TMCC, these layouts are large enough to accommodate at least three trains in action with others parked on yard tracks.

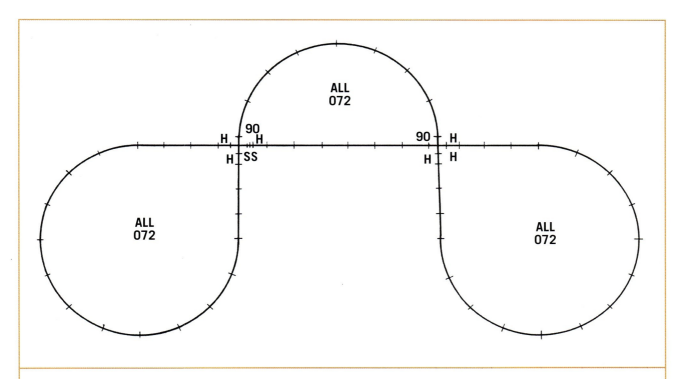

Even the largest Lionel locomotives will operate on the massive 072 curves on this double figure-8 layout. There's plenty of room to step over the tracks if the layout is assembled on the floor.

FASTRACK SECTIONS REQUIRED:

Quantity	Symbol	Part No.	Description
18	None	6-12014	10-inch Straight Track
32	72	6-12041	072 22 1/2-Degree Curved Track
2	90	6-12019	90-Degree Crossover
6	H	6-12024	Half-Straight
2	S	6102047350	1 3/8-inch Insulated Straight (furnished with 060 and 072 switches and as a replacement part; ballast shoulder on one side only)

SPACE REQUIRED: 10x19 feet

The Union Pacific 2-8-0 switches cars in the industrial siding while its train is parked on the inner passing siding. The Union Pacific passenger train is waiting at the station on the outer siding.

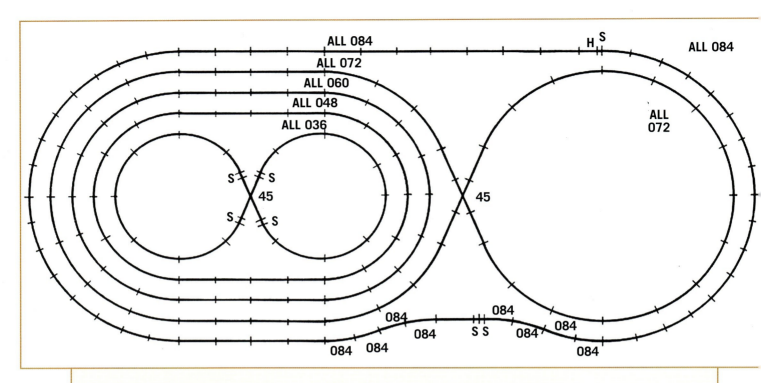

This five-train Christmas layout can be assembled on the floor or on a tabletop.

FASTRACK SECTIONS REQUIRED:

Quantity	Symbol	Part No.	Description
44*	None	6-12014	10-inch Straight Track
11	H	6-12024	Half-Straight
4	RU	6-12054	Operating Track
13	S	6102047350	1 3/8-inch Insulated Straight (furnished with 060 and 072 switches and as a replacement part; ballast shoulder on one side only)
12	36	6-12015	036 45-Degree Curved Track
12	48	6-12043	048 30-Degree Curved Track
16	60	6-12056	060 221/2-Degree Curved Track
28	72	6-12041	072 22 1/2-Degree Curved Track
40	84	6-12061	084 11 1/4-Degree Curved Track
1	45	6-12051	45-Degree Crossover

*Note: With the long straights on this layout you can substitute ten 30-inch Straight Tracks (6-12042) and fourteen 10-inch Straight Tracks (6-12014).

SPACE REQUIRED: 14x19 feet

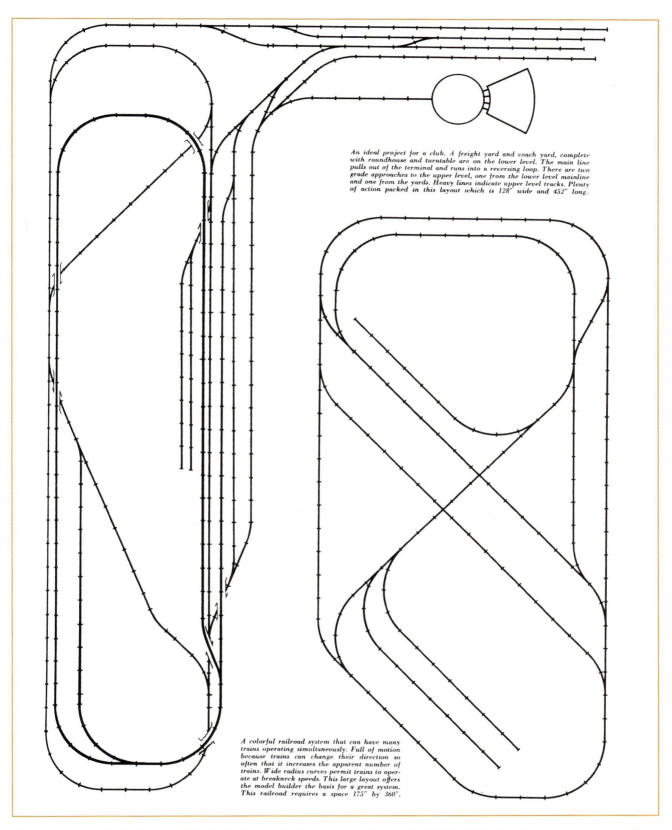

An ideal project for a club. A freight yard and coach yard, complete with roundhouse and turntable are on the lower level. The main line pulls out of the terminal and runs into a reversing loop. There are two grade approaches to the upper level, one from the lower level mainline and one from the yards. Heavy lines indicate upper level tracks. Plenty of action packed in this layout which is 128" wide and 452" long.

A colorful railroad system that can have many trains operating simultaneously. Full of motion because trains can change their direction so often that it increases the apparent number of trains. Wide radius curves permit trains to operate at breakneck speeds. This large layout offers the model builder the basis for a great system. This railroad requires a space 175" by 360".

The layout on the right will require 14 1/2x30 feet, while the layout on the left fills 10 1/2x38 feet. Both are designed for 072 curves and switches. *Courtesy Lionel LLC*

CHAPTER 12

Yard and Industrial Layouts

The real railroads use long lengths of a dozen or more parallel tracks to rearrange and to store individual cars. These groups of parallel tracks are called yards. On the real railroads, these parallel sidings usually have switches at both ends so the locomotives can move cars more easily. These are called through yards. Some very small railroads, as well as railroads that terminate at harbor piers or docks, may have rows of parallel tracks with switches only at one end and stub ends with bumpers at the opposite end of each track. These are usually called stub-ended yards.

FasTrack Railroad Yards

The three-track yards on these plans are actually self-contained layouts. The yards can, however, be used on larger layouts like the 14x19-foot shelf-style layout in Chapter 10. These yards are versatile because

A four-track through yard (the fifth track is the mainline) on Bill Langsdorf's layout. The downtown on the right is an assortment of Lionelville stores with an older Lionel Rico Station and four Illuminated Station Platforms (6-12748). The Pedestrian Walkover (6-14082) is at the end of station platform over Tracks 2 and 3. The train in the station on Track 2 is a partial Santa Fe Anniversary Set (6-21786) with four passenger cars. The train leaving the station on Track 3 is a Burlington Northern SD-60 MAC Diesel (6-18241) with five cars and a caboose. The train leaving the station on Track 4 is a dummy Burlington Northern SD-40 with a dummy Santa Fe Dash 8 and a Santa Fe–powered B Unit.

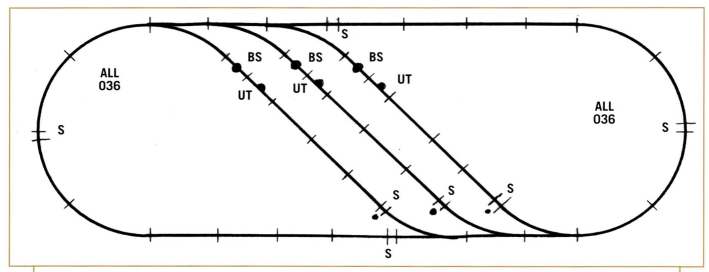

Three-track through yard layout.

FASTRACK SECTIONS REQUIRED:

Quantity	Symbol	Part No.	Description
17*	None	6-12014	10-inch Straight Track
3	BS	6-12060	Block Section (insulated half-straight)
7	S	6102047	350 1 3/8-inch Insulated Straight (furnished with 060 and 072 switches and as a replacement part; ballast shoulder on one side only)
3	UT	6-12020	Uncoupling Track
8	36	6-12015	036 45-Degree Curved Track
6	36	6-12046	036 Remote Switch (Right Hand)

*Note: With the long straights on this layout you can substitute five 30-inch Straight Tracks (6-12042) and two 10-inch Straight Tracks (6-12014).

SPACE REQUIRED: 3 1/2x9 1/2 feet

you can use them for either switching to rearrange trains or as simple storage tracks to hold complete trains. On these simple ovals, the yards allow you to run three trains, operating one while the other two rest in the yard. The diagonal arrangement also allows the tracks to be used as part of a reverse loop to change trains' directions. A train traveling counterclockwise around these layouts can only be reversed by backing it through the diagonal track.

Switching the Yard

The switching locomotive moves cars from one track to the next to assemble trains for specific destinations. The train may, for example, arrive at a yard in Philadelphia with some cars destined for New York

and other cars destined for Miami. The switcher uses two additional tracks, one for the New York–bound cars, the other for the Miami-bound cars. When enough cars were assembled for a full train, the switcher might add a caboose (prior to the 1970s). Then two road engines would be called to pick up their trains. Passenger trains were rearranged (the railroads' term is "switched") in a similar manner.

You can recreate all those operations with Lionel trains, thanks to the automatic couplers that are standard on most cars and locomotives. Most of the Lionel couplers have a small lever to manually pop open the knuckle, or you can lift one car just enough to disengage the coupler, then set it back on the rails. It's far more interesting, though, to uncouple by

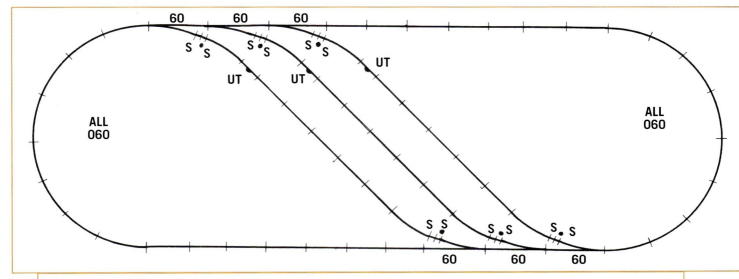

Three-track through yard layout.

FASTRACK SECTIONS REQUIRED:

Quantity	Symbol	Part No.	Description
29*	None	6-12014	10-inch Straight Track
3	BS	6-12060	Block Section (insulated half-straight)
12	S	6102047	350 1 3/8-inch Insulated Straight (furnished with 060 switches and as a replacement part; ballast shoulder on one side only)
3	UT	6-12020	Uncoupling Track
6	60	6-12058	060 Remote Switch (Right Hand)
22	60	6-12056	060 22 1/2-Degree Curved Track

*Note: With the long straights on this layout you can substitute seven 30-inch Straight Tracks (6-12042) and eight 10-inch Straight Tracks (6-12014).

SPACE REQUIRED: 5 1/2x15 feet

remote control. You will need a 6-12020 Uncoupling Track (designated RU on the plans) wherever you want to uncouple cars or locomotives by remote control. The couplers will, however, couple on any straight length of track. The 6-12054 Operating Track can also be used to uncouple cars and locomotives. If you operate a yard, you need at least three uncoupling tracks: one so the locomotive can be uncoupled from the incoming train and one on each of the two sidings to sort the cars from the incoming train.

Switching at Industries

The real railroads do most of their switching at individual industries where a single car (or a group of cars) is moved into the industry's railroad siding to be unloaded or loaded. Most of the plans in this book have stub-ended sidings to serve imaginary industries. Again, if you expect to be able to uncouple a car from the train to leave it at the industry, you need an uncoupling track. The plans in Chapter 2 show the ideal combinations of the 6-12054 Operating Track, 6-12020 Uncoupling Track, and the 6-12035 Lighted Bumper or 6-12059 Earthen Bumper. With Lionel accessories you can actually have industries that load or unload logs, coal, milk cans, ice, barrels, crates, mail bags, and other products.

Plans for Layouts with Yards and Industries

The classic plans that were published in the *Handbook for Model Builders* in 1940 included many

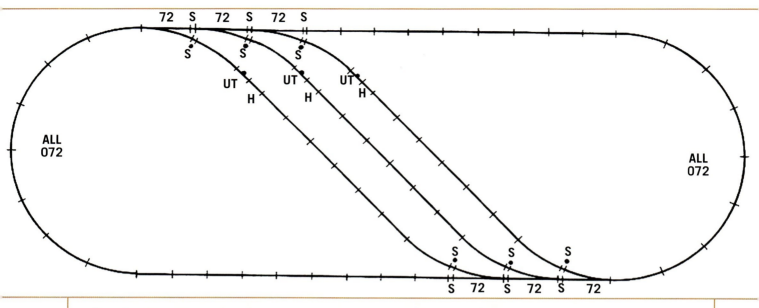

Three-track through yard layout.

FASTRACK SECTIONS REQUIRED:

Quantity	Symbol	Part No.	Description
36*	None	6-12014	10-inch Straight Track
3	H	6-12024	Half-Straight
12	S	6102047	350 1 3/8-inch Insulated Straight (furnished with 072 switches and as a replacement part; ballast shoulder on one side only)
3	UT	6-12020	Uncoupling Track
6	72	6-12049	072 Remote Switch (Right Hand)
22	72	6-12041	072 22 1/2-Degree Curved Track

*Note: With the long straights on this layout you can substitute twelve 30-inch Straight Tracks (6-12042).

SPACE REQUIRED: 6 1/2x18 1/2 feet

that featured multitrack yards and individual industrial sidings. You can recreate these plans with 072 FasTrack switches and curves, but you need to modify the plans or some of the track sections. FasTrack 072 switches include a short (1 3/8-inch) straight on the curved and straight routes that must be removed to make the FasTrack switches fit the plans. That also means that any track sections that join the diverging routes of 072 switches must be modified by

sawing off small sections of the ballast shoulders so they fit tightly into the 072 switch. The plans can be assembled in smaller spaces by removing pairs of straights from the opposite sides of the layout. These massive model railroads are the kinds of model railroads most of us just dream of. With FasTrack, however, you could assemble any of them on the floor of a basement den.

Opposite: Each of these four plans features a yard where you can make up and break down trains. The yards are stub-ended, except for a two-track yard on the bottom plan. All of the switches and curves are 072. The top plan is an expanded version of the loop-to-loop layouts in Chapter 8 and is layout is 9x34 feet. The second plan is 9x31 feet, a simple oval with the yard arranged along an inner passing siding. The third plan is 9x32 feet with a four-track yard, an offset oval, and a single reverse-loop connection. The bottom plan is 12x35 feet with the lower half double-track and two yards, one with three tracks and the other with two tracks.

"O-72" GAUGE TRACK LAYOUT IDEAS

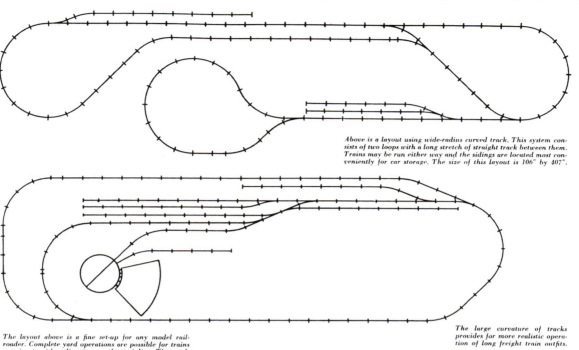

Above is a layout using wide-radius curved track. This system consists of two loops with a long stretch of straight track between them. Trains may be run either way and the sidings are located most conveniently for car storage. The size of this layout is 106" by 407".

The layout above is a fine set-up for any model railroader. Complete yard operations are possible for trains running in either direction on the mainline. The yards offer a good chance for a passenger terminal and freight handling. The engine terminal is large enough for complete yard equipment. Size is 107" by 367".

The large curvature of tracks provides for more realistic operation of long freight train outfits.

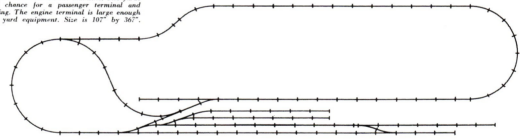

Below: Large layout having a real classification yard for freight rolling stock, and a turntable roundhouse with two lead-in tracks. The circular track in upper left corner may be concealed beneath a tunnel and used as a "sneak-off," so the same train is not continuously seen. Area 135" by 417".

Above: Another wide radius track layout having a single tracked mainline with a short-cut track for reversing. A large amount of yard trackage is shown. The bottom two sidings would make an ideal location for a terminal where trains may be relayed by means of a cross-over. Size is 98" by 374".

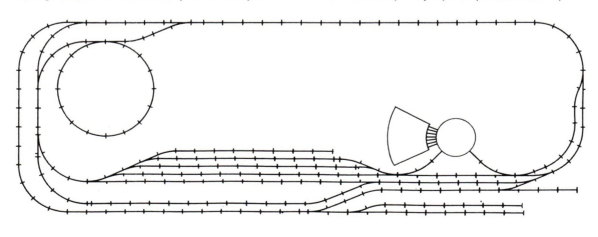

"O-72" GAUGE TRACK LAYOUT IDEAS

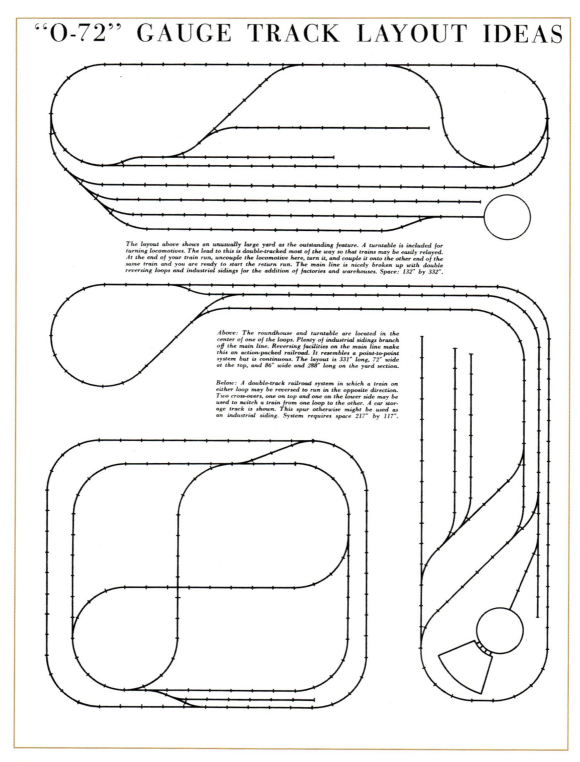

The layout above shows an unusually large yard as the outstanding feature. A turntable is included for turning locomotives. The lead to this is double-tracked most of the way so that trains may be easily relayed. At the end of your train run, uncouple the locomotive here, turn it, and couple it onto the other end of the same train and you are ready to start the return run. The main line is nicely broken up with double reversing loops and industrial sidings for the addition of factories and warehouses. Space: 132" by 332".

Above: The roundhouse and turntable are located in the center of one of the loops. Plenty of industrial sidings branch off the main line. Reversing facilities on the main line make this an action-packed railroad. It resembles a point-to-point system but is continuous. The layout is 331" long, 72" wide at the top, and 86" wide and 288" long on the yard section.

Below: A double-track railroad system in which a train on either loop may be reversed to run in the opposite direction. Two cross-overs, one on top and one on the lower side may be used to switch a train from one loop to the other. A car storage track is shown. This spur otherwise might be used as an industrial siding. System requires space 217" by 117".

These three plans are also designed for use with 072 curves and switches. The top plan is for an 11x28 foot area and can be considered as a six-track yard with a main-line oval that has reversing-loop cut-off tracks in both directions. The L-shaped plan is 28x24 feet with a three-track stub-ended yard and a triple-track main line. The bottom plan is for an 18x10-foot area with two separate loops but only a single yard track.

INDEX